THE FORGOTTEN GOSPELS

The Forgotten Gospels are the most significant texts outside the New Testament in terms of their early date, their otherwise unknown evidence on, and their perception of Jesus and Christianity.

It has long been acknowledged that some important and illuminating writings were omitted from the New Testament canon. Tim Newton has gathered together the key texts – newly translated from the Greek, Latin, Hebrew, Slavonic and Coptic – and written clear, concise and perceptive explanations of their origins and relevance. Together these comprise the historian's best resource to supplement the story of Jesus, his teachings and the beginnings of Christianity.

Tim Newton was educated at Cambridge. He is a classics scholar, Greek teacher and bibliophile. He lives in Devon.

THE FORGOTTEN GOSPELS

Life and teachings of Jesus
supplementary to the New Testament

A new translation

Edited and compiled by

Tim Newton

COUNTERPOINT

BERKELEY

To Amy, Stephanie, Matthew & Oak with love

Copyright © 2009 by Tim Newton
Counterpoint Press

First published in the UK by Constable,
An imprint of Constable & Robinson Ltd, 2009

Library of Congress Cataloguing-in-Publication Data
A CIP catalog record for this book is available from the Library of Congress

ISBN 978-0-78671-900-6

COUNTERPOINT
2117 Fourth Street
Suite D
Berkeley, CA 94710

www.counterpointpress.com

Distributed by Publishers Group West
Printed and bound in Italy

CONTENTS

CONTENTS

ACKNOWLEDGEMENTS

The editor wishes to express his thanks and appreciation to the Trustees of the Bodleian Library; and, for many kinds of generous help, to Sarah Portley and Becky Kent, my indefatigable and uncomplaining scribes; to Becky Hardie and Andreas Campomar, my editors; to Bill Fisher, Robert Simpson, Stephen Terry and Ben Lazarus; to Eli and Hannah, and lastly to Nick without whom . . .

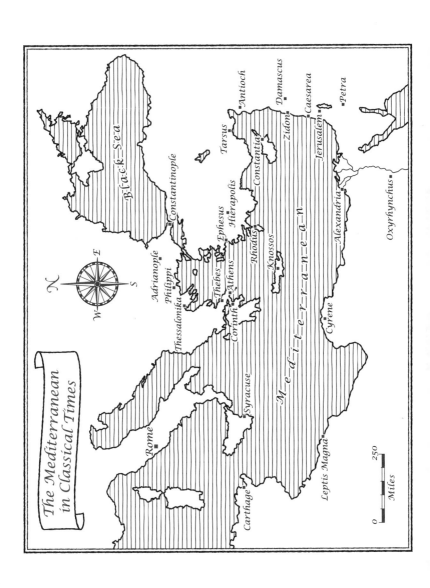

The Mediterranean in Classical Times

Rome
Carthage
Syracuse
Leptis Magna
Thessalonika
Adrianople
Philippi
Corinth
Thebes
Athens
Constantinople
Ephesus
Hierapolis
Tarsus
Rhodus
Knossos
Cyrene
Constantia
Zidon
Antioch
Damascus
Caesarea
Alexandria
Jerusalem
Petra
Oxyrhynchus

Black Sea
Mediterranean

N
E
S
W

0   250
Miles

PREFACE

The present volume is a consequence of the editor's desire to fill a vacuum in current non-academic Christian literature. There are many interesting texts from the beginning of Christianity not easily accessible to the lay reader, especially those not written by Christians. And nowhere are they to be found all in one place. The commanding position held by the New Testament has all but obliterated popular discussion of any other early Christian material. Yet these other texts deserve not to be forgotten.

By concentrating on the best and most pertinent for an understanding of early Christianity, the editor feels that the reader may escape that frustration and fatigue associated with the reading of ostensibly obscure or repetitive texts that are the exclusive province of scholars. These texts provide not only intriguing historical material but in small ways add to our knowledge of Jesus' teachings, if not the man himself.

Anyone choosing to study original Christianity outside the pages of the New Testament may do worse than start with the passages of text in the following compilation.

INTRODUCTION

One day in December 1945, two Arab peasants rode out on their camels to dig for natural fertilizer in the Nag Hammadi region of Upper Egypt. Beside a fallen boulder, one of them, Mohammed Ali, found a tall, red, sealed earthenware jar, buried deep in the earth. Afraid that it might contain a genie but simultaneously overcome by the excitement of buried treasure, he smashed it with his mattock. Out flew a mysterious golden dust . . .

So was made the discovery of the world-famous Nag Hammadi Library, thirteen ancient papyrus volumes – with some loose papyri soon to be used for kindling. This astonishing rescue of over fifty texts – thought to have been hidden in the second half of the fourth century when there was a purge of heretical doctrine – included as its ultimate prize the long-lost Gospel of Thomas, filled with unknown sayings and parables of Jesus.

Christian scholarship could take a further stride of understanding with this fund of new information. But it should not be denied that even the early Christian texts we have long possessed have yielded up many of their secrets with painful slowness. Perhaps we should consider these first.

At the heart of Christianity lies a body of miscellaneous documents collectively known as the New Testament. Everyone brought up within a Christian culture has some familiarity with them. But it is not usual to ask ordinary historical questions relating to them, such as: When were they written? For whom were they written? Who wrote them and why? And can they be relied upon for historical accuracy? Sadly, it is all too easy to merge them in a blur of extraordinary facts, esoteric doctrines and unconsidered authorship.

There is however a recognizable context in which they occurred. A remarkable man was born in the reign of the emperor Augustus about 7 BC, and grew up at Nazareth, a town of Galilee, a backward but fertile region north of Judaea. In the early AD 30s, for reasons still unclear to us, he died horribly by a traditional Roman method of execution, having shown proofs of his powers over the previous three or four years as a teacher and healer and even – so it was said – as a worker of miracles. This man made a huge impression upon certain of his followers who were determined to keep his teachings and memory alive.

It was deeply unfortunate for them that these doctrines were heretical in the eyes of orthodox Jews, and equally offensive to the Roman overlords who treated the strict separateness of the Christian religion (as with the Jewish one) as tantamount to atheism: for the Romans had a strongly enforced system of blending their own religion with those of their subject-states. This opposition was to lead to a multitude of troubles.

Over the next sixty years this remarkable group – among whom the chief apostle Peter, first Bishop of Rome, the dynamic convert Paul, James the first Bishop of Jerusalem, and John, last of the apostles, were the most prominent, according to our historical records – weathered all the storms they were exposed to. After the last of this generation was dead, there was an ever diminishing oral tradition directly linking Christians with those who had spoken to, and been instructed in person by, their leader, Jesus: the written records became increasingly important.

These records are of a motley kind. Chronologically, we begin with the letters of Paul – the first of these believed to have been written *c.* AD 50 to the Christians of Thessalonika in Greece. This earliest witness to Jesus is ironically the work of a man who had never known him, though he styled himself an apostle, like the twelve men elected by Jesus during his lifetime, and believed Jesus had once spoken to him in a famous episode on the road to Damascus. We might suppose the Book of Revelation to be the last in order, a fearsome and glorious vision of the future attributed to the aged apostle John *c.* AD 95.

These twenty-seven documents are assigned to a very small number of authors. Apart from Paul and John, there are Peter, James and Jude (James's brother), the writers of a few letters. And then there are the most important writers in the collection, the gospel authors.

They are named as Matthew (an apostle), Mark (a friend and companion of Paul and Peter), Luke (a doctor, and companion of Paul, who is also known for his account of the apostolic era), and John again, whose gospel is usually reckoned to be the last, perhaps close in date to his Book of Revelation and postdating the other three.

These 'gospels', whose Greek name corresponds to 'good news', are rightly considered the primary sources for an understanding of Jesus and his teaching. They scarcely cover more than a very short period at the end of his life, known as the Ministry, and are therefore limited as any kind of proper account of Jesus' life. Nevertheless, they unquestionably provide evidence for those events in which Christians would be most interested: Jesus' period of public service in the full view of society, when there were commonly at least a dozen witnesses to all his public actions, and often many, many more; and the extraordinary events immediately before and after his death.

Many doubts have surfaced, especially in recent years, about the authorship of these crucial documents and indeed of most of those gathered into the New Testament. For instance, Paul's letter to the Hebrews, while harmonious with the spirit of his other works, may very well be the work of another author; the name of his companion Barnabas has been proposed as a likely alternative.

The epistle of James, infused with the teachings of the Sermon on the Mount, and a true treasure of primitive Christianity, was perhaps written long after the first Bishop of Jerusalem's death. And there are frequent attempts to divide the authorship of the five works assigned to the apostle John: perhaps his gospel and first epistle[1] are the most likely to be authentic, though there is no escaping the huge problem posed by the apparent existence of a second John, also of Ephesus (in modern-day Western Turkey), whose tomb was also separately identified from the apostle's in the third century.[2] This may be John the elder – named by Papias, Bishop of Hierapolis, but in such a way as to leave a doubt whether he is actually the same person as the apostle. In respect of the authorship of the gospels, we should therefore be wary of taking attributions on trust without falling prey to that excessive scepticism that denies personal or recognizable authorship at all.

We might begin by considering the circumstances in which the gospels were written. The steady growth of Christianity, in the face not only of the hostility of the Jews and Romans but of other religious groups, was a remarkable event of the quarter of a century following Jesus' death. But the AD 60s witnessed shellshock after shellshock for the Christian community.

First James, reputedly Jesus' brother and a truly revered figure in the Jerusalem landscape, was murdered by the Jews in AD 62 for not repudiating Jesus. Then, just two years later, came the abominable assault by the emperor Nero upon the Roman Christians, during which persecution their leader Peter also seems to have died. Then, in AD 66, began the Jewish rebellion against the Romans, during which time the remaining Jerusalem Christians fled to Pella in Peraea. And somewhere about this time Paul also met a violent end in Rome. Of the chief apostles only John survived in Asia, his brother James having been executed by Herod Agrippa in AD 42.[3] (See Acts 12.1–2.)

We simply do not know when the first gospel was written but we can approximate its date close to the fall and destruction of Jerusalem in AD 70. Agreeing with modern scholarship, we now consider Mark's gospel as our primary text, a view at odds with that unanimously expressed by the earliest Christians.

For them, Matthew's was certainly the first gospel. So, for example, our important witness, Papias, writing *c*. AD 125, notes that 'Matthew composed the sayings in Hebrew. And each person interpreted them according to his ability.' Eusebius, much later, elaborates this account by telling us that Matthew left behind a written document for the Hebrews when he had decided to take his teaching elsewhere.

But the wholesale adoption of Mark's gospel by both Matthew and Luke – 600 of Mark's 660 verses are also to be found in Matthew – and the adherence to Mark's order of events speak volumes for Mark's priority.

Mark's gospel is referred to by Papias at length, quoting 'the elder' as his source – meaning John the apostle (or that other John): Mark is said to have recorded Peter, including as much as he could remember of Peter's teachings, which he set down in an unsystematic way, as accurately and completely as he could.

It is possible to explain the discrepancy between modern and ancient thinking by our recognition that Matthew's original writing was composed in Judaea, while Mark's was far away in Rome; if Matthew's gospel began as a collection of sayings and took on the 'dress' of Mark's gospel, both might legitimately claim a kind of chronological priority, on different grounds. Perhaps the Gospel of Thomas, in this volume, gives us a sense of the original Matthew text.

But the first surviving continuous account of Jesus is certainly Mark's. So we must now briefly regard the startling statements supposed to have been made by Clement of Alexandria *c.* AD 200. An eighteenth-century transcript of what claims to be one of his lost letters informs us that, after Peter's death (*c.* AD 64), Mark left Rome for Alexandria, taking writings of his own and of Peter's, from which he subsequently designed additions to his first gospel to create 'a more spiritual gospel for us by those who have been perfected', i.e. for initiates.

While it is not really possible to say with absolute confidence whether this letter is genuine (suddenly recorded a millennium and a half after publication), it would offer an explanation for certain features of Mark's gospel, if we reverse Clement's order and so place the initiates' gospel chronologically before the standard, and therefore abridged version. But the gifted Clement would also have seen the need for a reversed order, and yet he does not comment on this. Nevertheless, we need not doubt that the gospel tradition in terms of settings, events and actions – the narrative structure, rather than sayings alone – can be traced to Mark, and the period he spent with Peter, in which the forthcoming gospel was surely discussed by them. Then, perhaps, it was published in its current form *c.* AD 65 at Rome, shortly after Peter's death or even in Peter's lifetime with his blessing, if we follow Clement of Alexandria. Mark's gospel reflects a wish to preserve in written and therefore permanent form some facts about Jesus' life at a time when the violent deaths of the apostles and other tragedies were overwhelming Christians, one consequence of this being the break-up of the oral tradition that had a direct connection with Jesus.

A late story told by Tyrannius Rufinus *c.* AD 404 places the apostles together after Pentecost on the point of setting out to instruct the world: in this meeting they are alleged to have agreed on the first 'creed', a shorthand set of Christian beliefs. While the story is not convincing as fact, it has its own interest as recognition of the search for consensus among the apostles. Eusebius mentions a similar get-together after the death of James, Bishop of Jerusalem, in AD 62, including the surviving apostles and Jesus' own family members (of whom most were still living); as a result of which Symeon son of Clopas was elected second Bishop. Would they not have discussed doctrinal problems? At such a moment it is natural to think of intense discussion among the Christian leaders over areas of dispute. One generation after Jesus' death, the need for formulated and permanent expressions of 'correct' points of view would be greater than ever. As well as the creeds and liturgies, the gospels could provide orthodox and even accurate information. But how accurate was the gospel information?

One of the great virtues of the gospels – something of a hallmark of their integrity, though we cannot be sure to what extent each writer thought his own work might displace others' – is their failure to produce a text consistent with those already available. The natural conclusion is that a later gospel-writer might feel able to set aside or alter sundry portions of an earlier text, either because he felt his own information was better or for pious reasons (from which causes Matthew commonly corrects Mark).

Luke's contradiction of Matthew upon the issues of Jesus' birth and genealogy provides two obvious examples of factual discrepancy. But here it is likely that, at the time of Luke's writing, he was unaware of Matthew's version: Luke is believed to be the third of the gospel-writers but only drawing directly upon the first of his predecessors.[4]

Later tradition has him writing his gospel in Greece, where he is supposed to have gone after Paul's death (c. AD 67?) and lived into old age.

Intricate charts have already been and will continue to be constructed demonstrating the complex connections between the first three gospels. Mark is considered a main source of the other two, along with further sources unique to each of Matthew and Luke. One is bound to think of Luke's words at 2.19 and 2.51: 'But Mary kept all these things, and pondered them in her heart' and 'but his mother kept all these sayings in her heart'. What clearer indication could there be of Jesus' mother as a source that Luke employed, whether or not they actually met?

It is Luke also who opens his gospel with the surprising words: 'Forasmuch as many have taken in hand to set forth in order a declaration of those things . . . believed among us . . .' By which he surely indicates a multitude of documents in circulation at the time of writing, of which only Mark's and Matthew's gospels now survive.

It is likely that, as with the writings of Peter supposedly taken by Mark to Alexandria, many important texts have disappeared, though not necessarily of equal value with those that we possess. These might have included notes kept by the apostles. Occasionally, a source illuminates itself, as with a comparison between Luke 11.39–41 and Matthew 23.25–26: the Luke passage introduces a peculiar mention of 'alms-giving' where a reference to 'cleansing' might be expected and is found in the parallel passage in Matthew. The solution to this puzzle appears to be a straightforward confusion between the Aramaic word for 'give alms' (*zakkau*) and that for 'cleanse' (*dakkau*): Luke or his source has simply misunderstood the original from which he is working.

Whether references to the 'wisdom of God' in Luke should also be seen as accidental relics of an older text is more open to question. Jesus twice refers to 'her', to quote from her at 11.49 ff and to indicate elsewhere, that she is 'justified of all her children'. This Judaic goddess-figure is strangely incongruous in doctrinal terms, and it is no wonder that Matthew chooses to omit her when introducing a similar quotation.

These writings – despite serious limitations that include Mark's failure as a geographer, and a tendency, especially in Mark and John, to blacken the Jews while lessening the culpability of the Romans[5] – should leave us in no doubt of their fundamental authenticity. There seems also no strong reason to deny the traditional ascriptions to their authors, with the exception of Matthew, whose original collection of sayings may have been worked into other material, especially Mark's, by another hand.[6]

I am hesitant to use the prophetic material found in the first three gospels (e.g. Luke 21) as any kind of argument for dating purposes. Here it is possible to take the view that the writers are being wise after the event, for the destruction of Jerusalem (AD 70) is a frequent theme, and the gospels are very close to this date. (But the writers never relish the success of any prophecy). It is at least as likely that the prophecy is genuine, whether through Jesus' psychic power or political acumen. It is also probable that certain statements have been coloured by future events: did Jesus really, as at Matthew 16.24, bid his disciples take up their crosses? However, the moving utterance that Jesus makes to Peter at the end of John's gospel (21.18–19)[7] should be entered as a caveat against prejudging this complex issue.

John's gospel is perceived as radically distinct from the other three, known collectively as the synoptic gospels. His vision of the *Logos*, or Word of God, made manifest in the person of Jesus, forms the striking prologue to a version of Jesus' ministry and death which lays stress upon the eternal truths that Jesus embodies. Jesus' dialogue with Pilate is a good example of this, turning as it does from the subject of an earthly kingdom to something more enduring and potent, by which Pilate is left dumbfounded (18.33–38). The factual material is often new, and there is an old tradition recorded by Eusebius that John, who had hitherto relied upon teaching by word of mouth, sought to fill in details of the Ministry up to the time of John the Baptist's arrest, beginning with the marriage at Cana that might even have been his own. Scholarship, which previously saw in this gospel the most Hellenized material, has lately detected traces of Aramaic originals capable in part of presenting this gospel as containing information of real antiquity, despite its apparent lateness of date (*c.* AD 90?). Surely the intense vividness of Peter and John's arrival at the empty tomb on the morning of the resurrection (20.2–8) can only be the work of an eyewitness?

But the situation is further complicated by gospel transmission. We have hundreds of early New Testament fragments, and complete texts also, beginning with the tiny Rylands fragment, found in Egypt and dated to the first quarter of the second century: this gives a portion of John 18.31–38 and astonishes us by its distance from its Ephesian original in so short a time.[8] But do not imagine we are so lucky as to find them all in agreement.

The early eighteenth-century scholar John Mill knew of 30,000 variant readings, and it is plain that a great many of these are not the result of inaccuracy: there were genuine differences of textual material. Picking our way through this minefield, we are nowadays inclined to lean upon two early and significant codices still surviving. These are the *Codex Sinaiticus* and *Vaticanus*, both dating from *c.* AD 325; the *Codex Bezae*, of a somewhat later date, has a special interest for numerous passages at variance with the orthodox text.

We might start with the ending of Mark's gospel. Our early manuscripts do not support a belief that this extended beyond verse eight of chapter sixteen, ending: 'they trembled and were amazed: neither said they anything to any man; for they were afraid'. This powerful ending – of the women baffled by the mystery of the empty tomb – was not deemed sufficient to the miracle of the resurrection, though it fits well with Mark's plain-spokenness and omission of the miraculous birth. Therefore a leading Christian – identified in an early manuscript as Aristion, presumably one of 'the disciples of the Lord' whose words of teaching ranked with John the elder's (when Papias was a young man at the end of the first century) – undertook to summarize the events that followed.

This task he performed precisely if perfunctorily in the last twelve verses, as if he was not willing to intrude more than was absolutely necessary upon the work of his predecessor. But oddly, at verse 14, where Jesus appears for the first time to the eleven, we find an alternative longer version, in which the apostles seek to defend themselves from Jesus' accusation of disbelief and are answered by a warning of impending troubles. Known as the *Freer Logion* (from an American purchaser of a manuscript containing it – and the Greek for 'saying'), this was also familiar to Jerome. We cannot really account for it except as a further pious addition by another early hand, for the language, of an unusually apocalyptic kind, is considered inconsistent with what precedes and follows.

More remarkable still is the sentence that may once have formed part of the Lord's Prayer. The early second-century heretic Marcion, among others, adds at Luke 11.2: 'Let thy holy spirit come upon us and cleanse us.' It has been suggested that 11.13 – referring to God's gift of the Holy Spirit – makes much more sense with this addition.[9]

The story of the woman taken in adultery presents another set of problems. We know that the story in John's gospel (John 7.53–8.11) has probably been added from elsewhere, being unsupported by our best Greek manuscripts. Now Eusebius informs us that both Papias and the Gospel of the Hebrews included this story, without his indicating which he considers to be the original source.

An Armenian manuscript preserves a secondary version, with two important differences. Jesus writes in the earth 'to declare their [the accusers'] sins, and they were seeing their several sins on the stones'. After they have departed 'ashamed', Jesus does not condemn the woman but instructs her to 'present the offering for sins'. Later, Augustine was to claim this story as troublesome to some, who, fearing it was a licence for women's adultery, actually omitted it. From another point of view, it is a unique incursion of apocryphal literature into the New Testament. In some manuscripts, it is found at Luke 21.38, where it appears to fit more satisfactorily than in the corresponding place where it is found in John.[10]

There are many other interesting, if not necessarily important, differences. At Matthew 10.23 the *Codex Bezae* adds: 'and if they persecute you in the other [city], flee to a third'. The theologian Roderic Dunkerley stresses here the idea of persistent persecution and the need for endurance. Likewise the same *Codex* adds: 'this day have I begotten thee . . .' at Luke 3.22, concluding the speech from heaven, when the Holy Ghost descends on Jesus. This is found in the Gospel of the Ebionites and is a quotation from the Psalms.

It is certainly interesting to note that quite a number of manuscripts carry the first name of 'Jesus' for the insurgent and murderer Barabbas (who perhaps formed a part of a popular uprising when Jesus entered Jerusalem). Origen had also found this and possibly carries the tradition of this name back into the first century. Jesus (or Joshua) was a common name, but we can understand why it might have been discounted.

At Luke 23.48, the words of the breast-smiting mourners at the crucifixion are found in some early manuscripts: 'Woe to us for our sins; for the desolation of Jerusalem hath drawn nigh.' This is itself a variant of a text in the Gospel of Peter, from which perhaps it is drawn (see 'Other Texts').

One last example comes from Luke's account of the scene in the garden of Gethsemane immediately before Jesus' arrest. Scholars have been fascinated by Luke 22.44, where Luke states: 'And being in agony he prayed more earnestly: and his sweat was as it were great drops of blood falling down to the ground.' Here, the interest lies in understanding that, while the mid-second-century Justin knew these words, Clement of Alexandria some fifty years later did not. They became a battleground to prove Jesus' humanity to those who doubted it (the Docetists), and their presence – where present – in the original text became a central plank of the 'humanist' point of view. To this day, the strong possibility remains that they are an interpolation, while another opinion proposes them as evidence that Jesus suffered from the rare condition of haematidrosis, in which blood vessels rupture to give the appearance of sweating blood.[11]

At such a distance from these events we are entitled to ask: does any of this matter? The answer is a decisive *yes*. We need to be clear, so far as we can, about what really happened so long ago, not only because of current belief systems based on Jesus' teachings but because of our recognition that these teachings could not function in a void. We need to acquire the clearest ideas about the man responsible for them and the times in which he lived, and so enable ourselves to measure his calibre as best we can, by recourse to all the evidence at our disposal.

Our New Testament documents, for all their worthy intentions, should be recognized as propaganda, and not therefore bound to record every wart and wrinkle. They were chosen with care by many panels of judges, while many other similar texts were discarded. But any short review of surviving documents will indicate how far they chose themselves because of the inadequacy of their rivals.

The first attempt at a canonical list was drawn up by the heretic Marcion about AD 140. He looked only to Luke's gospel and Paul's letters, and not even these in their complete form. Our first significant list, however, is preserved in very carelessly transcribed Latin and estimated to have been prepared about forty years later. It is called the Muratorian fragment and runs in part as follows: '. . . [talks of Peter?] at which however he [Mark?] was present and so he has recorded [them?]. The third gospel book, according to Luke: this doctor Luke after Christ's ascension, since Paul had taken him along as one devoted to the law [teaching?], wrote it in his own name, as he thought proper. But neither did he see the Lord in the flesh, and therefore as he was able to ascertain it, so he begins the story at the birth of John. The fourth of the gospels, of John a disciple: At the urging of his fellow-disciples and bishops, he said, "Fast with me today for three days and let us each relate to one another whatever is revealed to us." The same night it was revealed to Andrew one of the apostles that, whilst all should check it, John should record everything in his own name . . .' (There follows a list of further canonical and excluded works, in which we find as acceptable the Wisdom written by Solomon's friends – as well as Peter's Apocalypse.)

Justin had already accepted at least three of the four gospels in the mid-second century and Irenaeus all of them before the end of it. However, opinion still remained divided on Luke's, and far more serious doubts clung to John's some way into the third century. Eusebius' classification into three groupings – accepted, disputed, spurious – was another step forward. And finally our current New Testament was treated as exclusively canonical by Athanasius in AD 367 – a decision ratified by the Synod of Carthage thirty years later.

However useful this was for establishing an orthodoxy of belief, it would be wrong to assume the worthlessness of the rejected literature. The present volume is intended as a reminder that certain other early texts also deserve real consideration.

Turning now to the non-canonical gospel materials included in the present volume, we are bound to note certain contrasts with the gospels of the New Testament. First, all of these inclusions were localized: that is to say, they belonged to particular Christian communities, so far as we can tell; even the Secret Gospel of Mark which, if it really existed, might be justly reckoned the most important Christian document ever written, was perhaps known only in Alexandria.

Second, with the exception of the Secret Gospel, we are probably correct in believing that they were all ultimately rejected. In other words, they were deemed inferior to those in the New Testament.

Lastly, except for the Gospel of Thomas, they survive only in fragmented form. This means in consequence that, lacking most internal clues, we are involved in a more considerable struggle over details of authorship and composition. Nor does tradition – of some real benefit respecting the New Testament gospels – prove as useful as we might hope: there was simply not enough interest in these documents, among the scholars and historians of the church, whose attitude was scarcely likely to be favourable to them. Only the heresiologists, hunting false doctrine to oppose and crush it, were regularly disposed to mentioning certain texts veering from the orthodox.

All the gospel fragments present here can be confidently assigned to at least the second century, and in most cases to the early part of that century if not earlier still. We have seen the Rylands fragment of John's gospel dated to *c.* AD 125, but this is by no means necessarily earlier than Papyrus Egerton 2 in the British Library, containing fragments of a non-canonical gospel thought to be derived from an independent oral tradition (see 'A Second Unknown Gospel'). Another manuscript considerably less old contains a striking episode from another unknown gospel, encouraging in almost all its detail our belief that this is a genuine lost story from the life of Jesus (see 'An Unknown Gospel').

The Gospel of the Hebrews, which Jerome went to the trouble of translating wholly or in part, may be dated to the time of the canonical gospels, if we accept that a quotation in the writings of Ignatius (died *c.* AD 107) is taken from it. This quotation concerns the fear felt by the apostles when confronted for the first time by the risen Jesus, who they evidently thought might be a ghost – a rather natural human reaction to that extraordinary situation. A more intriguing deviation from the gospels is the resurrection appearance to James the Just straight after Jesus' leaving the tomb, having 'given the linen to the servant of the Priest'. This appearance, though recorded by Paul, is in a radically different place in the sequence.

In the Gospel of the Nazareans the colourful arrival of the Magi and their retinue – it would be odd indeed if they came without servants – also reflects a variant account while, much more remarkably, we seem to touch upon the earliest tradition concerning Jesus' relations with John the

Baptist – how in opposition to his own family, Jesus was most unwilling to go and be baptized by him.

The esoteric nature of Jesus' dialogue with Salome, on women and sexuality – of which a tiny portion survives from the Gospel of the Egyptians – hints at the possibility of teachings radically distinct from our New Testament texts. Whether this apparent Gnosticism is really to be derived from Jesus or its unknown author is not clear, but the language is unquestionably impressive.

A quotation from another part of this dialogue is also apparently to be found in the Gospel of Thomas (Saying 61). This remarkable work, which was only recently redis-covered (among the Nag Hammadi Library) in its complete form, is a major addition to Christian literature, consisting of some 150 sayings attributed to Jesus. These, including two unknown parables and also many other texts uncon-nected with the New Testament, convey an intense vision of the immediate presence of the Kingdom. This gospel's near-failure to survive is somewhat mysterious.

Moving on to the non-gospel texts of various kinds, we observe the great variety of writers with information to place before us, some of the same vintage as the gospel-writers – the rabbi Samuel the Small, Clement Bishop of Rome, Ignatius of Antioch and Mara bar Serapion.

Quadratus, the first apologist, remembers how people (whom perhaps he had met) had survived till recent times after being long before healed by Jesus. Papias, Bishop of Hierapolis in Asia Minor, whose work is an inestimable loss, cites a long and fantastic vision of the coming kingdom put forward by Jesus and disbelieved by Judas Iscariot. Hegesippus, the Christian traveller, describes the life and cruel death of James the Just, called Jesus' brother; and a first-century interview conducted by the emperor Domitian with Jesus' great-nephews to see if these harmless small-holders posed any threat to him.

Tacitus, the famous historian, recounts the horrors perpetrated upon the Christians after the great fire at Rome in AD 64 – horrors of which he does not really disapprove. Josephus tells of an Egyptian prophet who preached on the Mount of Olives and marched into Jerusalem with his followers to make himself ruler, within some twenty years of Jesus' death. There are question marks over the authenticity of his sympathetic account of Jesus and, likewise, over some extraordinary variant texts of his writing preserved in Slavonic which mention *inter alia* how Pilate was responsible for a massacre at the time of Jesus' (first) arrest and accepted a huge bribe from the Jews.

The Talmud records the execution of Jesus forty days after a herald announced that he was to be stoned for sorcery and other crimes, but that a defender might come to plead for him. It also denies his legitimacy, as more vigorously does Celsus, the second-century Platonist, who believes

Mary had an affair with a soldier called Panthera and fled to give birth in secret (this perhaps accounting for Jesus' birth in Bethlehem, not Nazareth). And Clement of Alexandria, the Christian philosopher, records the aged John trekking into the mountains to rescue a young ex-Christian robber-chief from the error of his ways – and the courageous, tired old apostle is seen one final time responding so movingly to an audience wearied by his repetitiveness.

These additions to our knowledge of earliest Christianity are, of course, of varying interest and value. I am not willing to suggest that any one of them is indispensable. But it is a shame how far they tend to be neglected. I am sure I am correct in believing they can be enjoyed by a contemporary readership. The rise of Christianity out of unpromising and savage circumstances is one of the most remarkable stories of the world. Here you may find some lesser-known pieces of that story.

I

AN UNKNOWN GOSPEL

From the following gospel fragment we may feel entitled to speculate how much more was probably known in early times about Jesus' ministry, quite separate from the New Testament (NT) writings. Here Jesus springs to life in an episode of which we have no other record.

In the sands of Oxyrhynchus, anciently the chief town of a district of Lower Egypt (and now Behnesa), the tireless archaeological partnership of Bernard Grenfell and Arthur Hunt made a spectacular discovery in 1905. Their find was a tiny parchment leaf, less than nine centimetres square, written on both sides in microscopic Greek lettering. This was thought to have been used as an amulet, a portion of a fifth- or sixth-century copy of a work originally written perhaps as early as the second century.

The content of the text describes two episodes set in Jerusalem. In the first, Jesus warns his followers to protect themselves from becoming evil-doers with ensuing dire consequences. In the second, he goes with his disciples to the

1. ... Before doing wrong he practises every kind of deception. But pay attention that you do not also experience suffering similar to theirs.

For not only among the living do evil-doers among men receive their due but they also submit to punishment and much torment.

2. And he took them and led them into the very place of purification, and was walking around in the Temple. And a certain Pharisee, a chief priest named Levi, met with them and addressed the Saviour: 'Who permitted you to walk this holy place and see these holy vessels without your washing or your disciples having bathed their feet? But you have walked in this temple, in its purity, defiled, which no one else walks in unless he has bathed and changed his clothes; not does he dare to look upon these holy vessels.' And at once the Saviour stood still with his disciples and answered him:

'So what about you here in the temple, are you clean?' He said to him, 'I am. For I washed in the pool of David and went down by one stair and came up by the other; and I put on white, clean clothing, and after that I came and looked upon these holy vessels.'

The Saviour said in answer to him: 'Woe to you blind who do not see. You have washed in these running waters, where dogs and pigs[1] have been left day and night, and you have cleansed and wiped the outer skin, which prostitutes also and flute-girls[2] anoint and smooth and rub and beautify to arouse men's desires: but within they are filled with scorpions and every kind of wickedness. But I and my disciples, who you say have not bathed, have been immersed in the waters of eternal life that come from ... But woe unto the ...

27

Temple court, where he meets a Pharisee who criticizes him for not observing cleansing rituals in a holy place. This clearly enrages Jesus, who proceeds to contrast outer cleanliness with the true inner cleanliness that distinguishes him and his disciples (a theme also to be found in Matthew 23.27 ff).

The author is well informed about Temple practices, and his text contains numerous expressions of Jewish origin. This is our only surviving fragment of a gospel perhaps to be ranked as on a par with the synoptic gospels.

II

A SECOND
UNKNOWN GOSPEL

In the passages from the following gospel we see how non-standardized even familiar stories about Jesus remained for many years after the four main gospels were written. Among these garbled versions, one may observe for instance in the last extract the incident leading to Jesus' famous response: 'Render unto Caesar what is Caesar's . . .'

The fragments of this gospel, preserved in British Library Papyrus Egerton 2 and consisting of scarcely more than two leaves written on both sides, are dated to the first half of the second century. The author shows familiarity with all four gospels, leaning upon John for much of the language of the first episode, in which Jesus appears to be on trial, perhaps for violating the Sabbath; and on the synoptics for the following two episodes. A fourth incident is not reproduced here as it is in a very poor condition, but it evidently concerns a scene beside the river Jordan: Jesus asks a question involving the mystery of the resurrection and answers it himself with a miracle of the ripening of a grain of seed immediately after sowing.

1. And Jesus said to the Lawyers, 'You punish everyone who transgresses the law but not me . . .' And turning to the rulers of the people he spoke as follows: 'You search the scriptures in which you suppose you have life: these are the same bearing witness to me. Do not imagine that I came to accuse you to my father! Moses is your accuser, he in whom you have placed your hopes.'

And when they said, 'We are quite aware that God spoke to Moses, but we do not know where you are from,' Jesus answered them with these words, 'Now are you accused for your unbelief . . .'[1]

2. They took counsel with the crowd to gather stones together and stone him. And the rulers laid their hands upon him to seize him and hand him over to the crowd. But they could not seize him because the hour of his betrayal had not yet come. But the Lord himself escaped out of their midst and turned away from them. And behold a leper approached and spoke to him: 'Master Jesus, who move in the company of lepers and dine with them in the inn, I also have leprosy. If then you will it, I shall be made clean.' And the Lord said to him, 'I will it: be cleansed.' And at once the leprosy left him. And the Lord said to him, 'Go and show yourself to the priests . . .'

3. They approached him in a sceptical spirit to test him with these words: 'Master Jesus, we know that you have come from God. For the things that you do bear a witness to you that surpasses all the prophets. So tell us. Is it acceptable to pay to kings whatever their governing demands? Are we to pay them or not?'

But Jesus, perceiving their intention, spoke to them in rebuke: 'Why do you call me "Master" with your mouth but

These passages are really to be considered as variants on known texts but are fascinating as the 'working up' of material by memory, and perhaps oral tradition or even imagination. For it is reckoned that the author had no actual texts to work from at the time.

do not listen to what I say? Isaiah prophesied accurately concerning you when he said, "This people honours me with their lips, but their heart is far from me: they reverence me in vain . . .""

III

THE GOSPEL OF
THE EBIONITES

The orthodoxies of Christianity arrived slowly. In the fragmentary remains of the doctrines of the Ebionites – Jewish Christians, once followers of James, Jesus' brother – there are clearly Judaic features but also signs of early heresy in their refusal to accept Jesus as son of God and their acknowledgement of him as an archangel.

The citations from this gospel are entirely derived from the writings of Epiphanius, *c.* AD 315–403. Born in Palestine, he had founded a monastery by about the age of twenty, and became Bishop of Constantia in Cyprus in AD 367. He was a champion of Christian orthodoxy, taking issue with John Chrysostom and the great Origen (whom he declared a heretic in AD 394). His record of the Ebionites is, unsurprisingly, of a group opposed to the truth.

After the death of Jesus, his brother James became hugely prominent among the Christians (see Hegesippus) and was the first bishop of the Jerusalem church. His austerity, devoutness and integrity placed him in a special position with

Extract 1:

In the gospel used among them called according to Matthew though not whole and perfect, but bastardized and mutilated and called by them the Hebrew Gospel, it is reported as follows:

There appeared a man named Jesus, about thirty years of age, who chose us. And coming to Capernaum, he entered the house of Simon also called Peter, and opened his mouth to say, 'As I was passing by the lake of Tiberias I chose John and James, the sons of Zebedee, and Simon and Andrew and Thaddeus and Simon the Zealot and Judas Iscariot, and you Matthew I called as you sat in the custom-house, and you followed me.[1] You then I intend to be twelve apostles for a witness to Israel.'

Extract 2:

And after saying many things it carries on:

When the people had been baptized, Jesus also came and was baptized by John. And as he came up from the water, the heavens were opened, and he saw the Holy Spirit in the form of a dove descending and entering him. And a voice came out of heaven saying, 'You are my beloved son, in you I am well pleased.' And further: 'Today I have begotten you.'

And at once a great light shone about the place. Seeing this . . . John said to him, 'Who are you, Lord?' And again a voice resounded to him from heaven, 'This is my beloved son, in whom I am well pleased.'

And then . . . John fell down before him saying, 'I beg of you, Lord, baptize me.' But he stopped him, saying, 'Let it alone, for thus it is fitting for all things to be fulfilled.'

Extract 3:

They deny he was begotten by God the Father, saying he was created as one of the archangels . . . and rules over the angels and

Christians and Jews alike. After his death *c.* AD 62, only a few years passed till the destruction of Jerusalem by the Romans, and so, like the rest of the Jews, his followers were scattered.[2]

Sometime, at the beginning of the second century, a gospel was written for one of these groups of followers, possibly in the region east of Jordan – evidently based on Matthew's, and beginning with the ministry of John the Baptist, and omitting the nativity story. The author or authors also had access to the gospels of Mark and Luke, all three gospels providing source material for the story of Jesus' baptism (Extract 2).

The Ebionites denied the virgin birth, believing (Extract 2) in his mystical union with the Holy Spirit at the time of baptism; they were opposed to Temple cult practices – as with the sacrifices (Extract 3); probably vegetarian, they were strongly Judaic in outlook, with a strong element of Gnosticism (that tendency towards knowledge or 'Gnosis' of an internal and mystical kind, and repudiation of the flesh).

Eusebius, basing his information and opinions upon the third-century Origen's, derived the Ebionites' name from a word indicating poverty: this is probably a faithful representation of the lifestyle they had chosen in imitation of James. Eusebius says that they regarded Jesus as a man in all respects and believed implicitly in orthodox Jewish observances of the law.

But a second group, possibly a splinter from the first, accepted the nativity story, and while agreeing on the observances, rejected the writings of Paul. These were not the group among whom the Gospel of the Ebionites had its currency.

We do not know when this sect, in either of its forms, died out.

IV

THE GOSPEL OF
THE HEBREWS

This possibly Egyptian gospel offers another intriguing set of events and sayings at odds with the NT writings. While Jesus' conception and baptism are also markedly different, it is the graphic and precise nature of Jesus' appearance to James after the resurrection that cries out for our careful consideration.

Like the Gospel of the Nazareans and of the Ebionites, this was the main text of a group of Jewish Christians. These are quite likely to have been Egyptians, given that two of our main sources, Clement and Origen, were Alexandrians. It has been suggested that this gospel should be contrasted with the Gospel of the Egyptians, written for gentile Christians. As it was known to Hegesippus it may be dated to the beginning of the second century.

Because of the scanty nature of the texts, it is not easy to come to firm conclusions. The first passage suggests a very different account of Jesus' birth from the New Testament, and his baptism (2) is also distinct, in an

1. That one said, It is written in the Gospel according to the Hebrews that when the Christ wished to come upon the earth to mankind, the Good Father summoned a great power from the heavens, which was called Michael, and he entrusted the Christ to it. It came down to the world and was called Mary; he dwelt in her womb for seven months.

2. . . . but according to the gospel written in the Hebrew language that the Nazareans read: the whole font of the Holy Spirit will descend over him . . . Again in the gospel, of which we made mention above, we discover these things written: But it happened that when the Lord ascended from the water, the font of the whole Holy Spirit descended, and came to rest over him, and said to him: 'My son, I was waiting for you among all the prophets, that you would come, and I would come to rest in you.

Indeed, you are my rest, you are my firstborn son, who rules for all time.'

3. If one believes the Gospel according to the Hebrews, there the Saviour himself says, 'Just then, my mother the holy spirit, took me, and carried me away by one of my hairs to the mountain – the great Tabor . . .'

4. . . . as we also read in the Hebrew gospel, that the Lord says to the Disciples: 'And never,' he said, 'be happy, except when you see your brother in affection.'

5. . . . And in the Gospel according to the Hebrews that the Nazareans are accustomed to read, this is set among the greatest crimes: One who has depressed the spirit of his brother.

6. Also, the gospel which is named after the Hebrews, and was recently translated by me

unrealistic way. Jesus describes a part of his temptation in the next passage, while the fourth and fifth dwell on the true Christian theme of brotherly love.

But, with the sole exception of the often repeated saying to be found in the Gospel of Thomas (Saying 2) in variant form, none of the surviving passages can command our attention half as much as Jesus' appearance to James the Just after the Resurrection.

In this version, James has evidently made a vow at the Last Supper to abstain from food until Jesus has fulfilled a prophecy about his return from the dead. So Jesus comes to him after giving the linen cloth to the priest's servant – perhaps the young man in white, recorded at Mark 16.5? And is this person Malchus, whose ear Jesus healed (Luke 22.50–51) at the time of his arrest?[1]

An appearance to James is recorded by Paul (1 Corinthians 15.7) but towards the end of the sequence. Nevertheless, it shows a similarity to the appearance on the road to Emmaus, to Cleophas and another. If James could be identified with the apostle James the son of Alphaeus (= Cleophas?), perhaps he was the second person there with his father. He would also have been present at the Last Supper (as an apostle).[2] At any rate, we cannot doubt James' importance for this group of Christians.

There is also another text indicating the extreme nervousness felt by the apostles when first confronted by the into the Greek and Latin language, the one that Origen also often uses, says after the resurrection of the Saviour: But when the Lord had given the linen to the servant of the priest, he went to James and appeared to him. Indeed, James had taken an oath that he would not consume bread from that hour when he had drunk the wine-cup of the Lord, until he would see him rising from those that sleep. And again a little after: Bring, said the Lord, a table and bread. Straight after is added: He brought bread and blessed it, and broke it and gave it to James the Just and said to him: My brother, eat your bread, because the Son of man has risen from those that sleep.

risen Jesus. Its very early date – it is first recorded by Ignatius, Bishop of Antioch, who died *c.* AD 107 – suggests another variant tradition of the resurrection, perhaps also from the Gospel of the Hebrews. Jerome records that gospel as its source:

> For after the resurrection too, I know and believe that he was in flesh. And when he came to those around Peter, he said to them: 'Take hold, feel me and see, that I am not a bodiless spirit.' And immediately they took hold of him and they believed, being mixed with his flesh and spirits.*[3]

This heretical gospel with Gnostic tendencies seems to have had no great currency, though it was known to Jerome in the fourth century. We have evidence that it was nearly as long as Matthew's, but our surviving texts suggest a character strikingly independent of the New Testament. It is difficult to assess the extent of our loss.

---

* Compare Luke 24.37–40 where, however, they do not touch him.

V

THE GOSPEL
OF THE NAZAREANS

One of the hugely important moments in Jesus' life is when, coming to John the Baptist to be baptized, he is recognized by the Baptist as the Messiah. In an extraordinary tradition preserved only in the Gospel of the Nazareans, we are astonished to discover that he may not have wanted to go at all but was cajoled by his own family.

This gospel, for which there is evidence that it was originally written in Syriac or Aramaic, is closely related to the Gospel of Matthew, but only in a secondary, derivative way.

It was written in the early years of the second century, for Jewish Christians in Syria and, since Epiphanius and Jerome unite in saying it was current at Beroea (Aleppo) in Coelesyria, this is probably where it originated.

The gospel is considered substantially orthodox, and in harmony with Christian dogma. While the texts are for the most part hardly sensational, there are some noteworthy exaggerations; for instance, that many thousands of Jews

1. For the gospel entitled 'According to the Hebrews' reports as follows:

Joseph gazing out saw a crowd of travellers coming in a body to the cave, and he said, 'I will arise and go out to meet them.' And when he had gone out, Joseph said to Simon, 'Those men coming seem to me to be soothsayers. For, look, every moment they stare up into the heavens and enter into discussion. But they appear also to be strangers, since even their clothing is different from our own. For their attire is very rich, and their complexion more swarthy, and they have caps on their heads, and their garments seem to me smooth-textured, and they wear baggy trousers.

And, see, they have stopped, and are directing their attention towards me; and, see, they are starting to walk again in this direction.'

(By these words we are clearly shown that not only three men but a crowd of travellers came to the Lord, even though certain authorities definitely name the particular leaders of the same company as Melchus, Caspar and Phadizarda.)

2. And behold the mother of the Lord and his brothers were saying to him: John the Baptist baptizes for the forgiveness of sins: let us go and be baptized by him. But he said to them: What sin have I committed, that I ought to go and be baptized by him? Unless, perhaps, this thing that I have said is ignorance?

3. If your brother has sinned, he said, in word and has done enough for you, accept him seven times in a day. His disciple, Simon, said to him: Seven times in a day? The Lord answered, and said to him: And also, I say to you, up to seventy times seven times, because in the Prophets too, after they were anointed with the Holy Spirit, sinful talk* was found.

* Or, talk of sin

became believers after Jesus spoke from the cross; or that rays darting from Jesus' eyes caused terror and flight.

The delightful appearance of the Magi with their retinue is an unexpected bonus as being unrelated to Matthew's original version. We do not know its source, but the mention of Simon (? = Simeon in Luke 2.25–35) suggests a detailed alternative storyline.

4. It says: The other rich man said to him: Master, what good shall I do that I may live? He said to him: Man, act according to the laws and the prophets. He responded to him: I have done so. He said to him: Go, sell everything you possess, and share it with the poor, and come, follow me.

But the rich man began to scratch his head, and it did not please him. And the Lord said to him: How is it that you say: I have acted according to the law and the prophets? Since it is written in the law: Hold your neighbour as dear as yourself and behold many of your brothers and children of Abraham are covered with filth, and are dying from hunger, and your home is full of many goods, and not a thing comes out from it to them. And turning he said to Simon his disciple sitting before him: Simon, son of Jona, it is easier for a camel to go through the eye of a needle, than for a rich man to enter the kingdom of heaven.

5. However, in the gospel that was written in Hebrew letters, we read not that the curtain of the temple was split, but that the lintel of the temple, of wondrous size, toppled down.[*1]

---

[*] Or, was broken and divided

VI

THE GOSPEL
OF THE EGYPTIANS

In the remarkable fragments of Jesus' conversation surviving from this gospel, he presents a challenge to conventional points of view on women, childbirth and even, stepping outside the natural world with which we are familiar, on the nature of gender itself.

In the third book of Miscellanies, chiefly devoted to issues of marriage and sexuality, Clement of Alexandria is concerned with combating the Encratites[1] and other contemporary heretics including Julius Cassianus. These used a gospel of the Egyptians as an important source of their teachings. Epiphanius was later to claim in the fourth century that another heretical group, the Sabellians, also employed it; and Hippolytus (third century) likewise respecting the Naassenes.

The interesting quotations that he introduces from the gospel, about which he is ambivalent, almost exclusively relate to a conversation between Jesus and Salome (who figures in the gospels as a woman from the innermost circle

1. To Salome, who was asking, 'How long then will death have power?', the Lord said, 'As long as you women give birth,' not because life is evil and creating wicked, but to teach the arrangement according to nature.

2. For it is said that the Saviour himself declared, 'I came to make an end of the labours of the female sex.'

3. For when she said, 'I have done well then by not bearing children,' when birth was being taken as not necessary, the Lord responded, saying, 'Eat all plants, but do not eat one that has bitterness.'

4. As Salome enquired when the things of which she had asked would be known, the Lord said, 'Whenever you tread on the clothing of shame, and whenever the two become one and the male with the female sex is neither male nor female.'[2]

of devotees). This conversation must be somewhat older than Clement's time, since the second epistle of Clement of Rome (*c.* AD 150) quotes from it.[3]

The conversation turns on sexual incontinence and procreation in an apparently hostile way, so that Jesus' stance might be taken as anti-sexual. But Jesus looks for a stronger unifying of the genders after the 'trampling on the garment of shame' and we are led to understand that some kind of spiritual transformation is intended.

Since this is almost all we know of this gospel and we cannot even tell whether Salome's dialogue was an original part of it or preceded it, it is impossible to form a judgement of the content as a whole. It would be natural to suppose that the Gospel of Thomas' Saying 61 was a part of the dialogue and of the gospel too; in which case the themes were altogether more wide-ranging.

This gospel appears to belong to the early part of the second century and to be one of our more serious losses. The contents of Salome's dialogue are of an exceptional quality.

VII

THE GOSPEL OF THOMAS

It is sufficient to say of this gospel that no surviving early Christian text outside the NT canon is likely to be considered of comparable significance as an independent source for Jesus' teachings. It is the great Christian discovery of the twentieth century, with its wealth of previously unknown sayings and parables of Jesus.

Among the papyri discovered at Oxyrhynchus by Grenfell and Hunt, there were three of particular interest found a little more than a century ago, the first in 1897; these (nos. 654 and 655) contained a number of sayings ascribed to Jesus, some but not all showing similarities to gospel teachings, and all of very early date.

Whatever opinion scholars may have held at that time, the extraordinary discovery at Nag Hammadi, also in Egypt, in 1945 of a virtually complete Coptic manuscript of these sayings, changed everything. Here was the full text of a gospel attributed to Thomas, evidently a fourth-century copy of a Coptic translation of the Greek original. It was a collection of 114

These are the secret sayings spoken by the living Jesus and set down by Judas Thomas the twin.[1]

1. And he said: Whoever interprets these sayings accurately shall not taste death.

2. Jesus said: Let him who seeks not cease until he finds. And, finding, he will be troubled. And, troubled, he will marvel. And he will reign over all.

3. Jesus said: If your leaders tell you, See, the kingdom is in heaven, then the birds of heaven will be before you. If they tell you, It is in the sea, then the fish will be before you. But the kingdom is inside you and outside you. When you know yourselves you will be known; and you will know that you are children of the living father. But if you do not know yourselves, you live in poverty and you are poverty.

4. Jesus said: The man aged in his days will not hesitate to ask a little child seven days old about the place of life, and the man shall live. For many that are first shall be last and shall become a single one.

5. Jesus said: Know what is in front of you and what is hidden from you will be revealed. There is nothing hidden that will not be revealed.

6. His disciples questioned him, saying: Do you want us to fast? How shall we pray? Shall we give to charity? Shall we observe rules in our eating? Jesus said: Do not lie nor do what you hate. For all things are revealed before heaven. Nothing hidden will not be revealed, nothing covered will remain uncovered.

7. Jesus said: Blessed is the lion that the man eats, and the lion becomes man. Cursed is the man that the lion eats, and the lion becomes man.

sayings, but since some had been jumbled together, the number was nearer 150. Only about 40 per cent related to gospel texts. Of the remainder, some had been quoted by early Christian writers, but no author except for Hippolytus (AD 170–235), and perhaps Origen, had referred directly to the gospel by name.[2] It is difficult to avoid the inference that the gospel was little known.

These sayings, set in very limited contexts or none at all, propose a Jesus (never called Christ) whose utterances are oracular and mystical, aids to a personal kind of internal salvation. The message might be summed up: The kingdom is already here if you are able to perceive it and partake of it.

By reference to quotations that may be taken from the Gospels of the Hebrews and of the Egyptians, we are probably correct in believing this a mid- or late-second-century text. But some of the material may be much older, including two unknown parables in a raw and primitive form (97 and 98).

Scholarly debate has still much more to say on this remarkable text, but there could be no suggestion of its inclusion in the NT, due to its apparent lateness of date as much as its apparent farrago of sources. This is the outstanding compilation of a very focused and able Christian.

NB: Various small losses in this text have been made good where clearly identifiable.

8. And he said: Man is like a wise fisherman who cast his net into the sea and hauled it out filled with little fish. Amongst them the wise fisherman found a large, fine fish. He threw all the little fish back into the sea and had no trouble in choosing the large one. He who has ears to hear, let him hear.

9. Jesus said: Behold! A man went out to sow. He filled his hand with seed and scattered it. Some fell on the road, and the birds came and ate it up. Some fell on rock and did not take root nor produce heads of grain. Some fell on thorns which choked it; and the worms consumed it. And some fell on good soil: it produced a good crop, yielding sixty or one hundred and twenty per measure.

10. Jesus said: I have thrown fire upon the world. And behold! I stand guard by it until it blazes.

11. Jesus said: This heaven will pass away, and the heaven beyond it likewise. The dead do not live nor will the living die. In the days when you ate what is dead, you made it alive. When you come into the light, what will you do? When you were one, you became two. But when you become two, what will you do?

12. The disciples said to Jesus: We know that you will leave us. Who will be in charge after you? Jesus replied to them: When you are there, you shall go to James the Just, for whose sake heaven and earth came into being.

13. Jesus said to his disciples: Compare me to something: what am I like? Simon Peter answered: You are like a true messenger. Matthew answered: You are like a wise philosopher. Thomas answered: Master, I am completely unable to say what you are like. Jesus said: I am not your master. For you have drunk

from and become drunk with the bubbling spring that I poured out. And he withdrew with him and said three things to him. When Thomas returned to his companions, they asked him: What did Jesus tell you? Thomas answered them: If I tell you only one of the things he said, you will take up stones and stone me; and a fire that comes out of the stones will consume you.

14. Jesus said to them: If you fast you will bring sin upon yourselves, and, if you pray, you will receive condemnation, and, if you give charitably, you will hurt your spirits. If you go into a land, traversing its regions, eat what those who receive you put before you, and heal the sick among them. For you will not be defiled by what enters your mouth: it is what comes out that will defile you.

15. Jesus said: When you see someone not born of a woman, fall down upon your faces and worship. He is your father.

16. Jesus said: People may suppose I have come to impose peace on the world. They are not aware that it is conflicts I have come to impose: fire, sword, war. For there will be five in a house: there will be three against two, and two against three, father against son and son against father, and they will stand up each alone.

17. Jesus said: I shall give you what no eye has seen nor ear heard nor hand touched, what has not entered the human heart.

18. The disciples said to Jesus: Tell us what our end will be. Jesus said: Have you found the beginning then that you are looking for the end? For where the beginning is the end shall be. Blessed is he who will stand at the beginning: he will know the end and not taste death.

19. Jesus said: Blessed is he who existed before his being. If you become my disciples and listen to my words, these stones will be your servants. For you have five trees in Paradise, unchanging in summer or winter; and their leaves do not fall. He who knows them will not taste death.

20. The disciples said to Jesus: Tell us what the kingdom of heaven is like. He told them: It is like a mustard-seed, the smallest seed of all. But when it falls on cultivated soil, it puts out a great shoot and becomes a shelter for heaven's birds.

21. Mary said to Jesus: What are your disciples like? He answered: They are like little children living in a field that is not theirs. When the owners of the field come, they will say, give us our field back. They will strip off in front of them in order to return it to them, and will make restoration. So I say: If the master of the house knows that the thief is coming, he will keep watch before he appears and will not let him break into his house and steal his possessions. You then, be on guard against the world. Prepare yourselves powerfully that thieves cannot find a means to come at you. For it will happen as you are expecting. Let there be a person of understanding amongst you. When the grain ripened, he came quickly, sickle in hand, and harvested it. He who has ears to hear, let him hear.

22. Jesus saw some babies at the breast. He said to his disciples: These little ones being suckled are like those who enter the kingdom. They said to him, Then if we are babies, shall we enter the kingdom? Jesus told them: When you make the two into one, and the inside as the outside, and the outside as the inside, and the upper as the lower; and when you make male and female into a single one, so that the male will not be male

nor the female female; when you make an eye in place of an eye, a hand in place of a hand, a foot in place of a foot, an image in place of an image, then will you enter.

23. Jesus said: I shall choose you, one from a thousand and two from ten thousand. And they will stand as a single one.

24. His disciples said: Teach us of the place where you are, for we must go in search of it. He told them: Who has ears, let him hear. There is light within a man of light, and it sheds light for the whole world. If it sheds no light, there is darkness.

25. Jesus said: Love your brother as your soul: keep him as the apple of your eye.

26. Jesus said: You see the mote in your brother's eye, but not the beam in your own. When you take the beam out of your own

eye, then will your sight be sufficient to take the mote out of your brother's.

27. If you do not fast from the world, you will not find the kingdom. If you do not keep the Sabbath as Sabbath, you will not see the father.

28. Jesus said: I stood in the midst of the world and appeared in flesh to them. I found them all drunk and none of them thirsting. My soul was in pain for the sons of men for they are blind in their hearts and do not see. They came empty into the world and are seeking also to depart empty from it. But now they are drunk. When they have shaken off their wine, they will repent.

29. Jesus said: If the flesh has come into being because of the spirit, it is a wonder. But if the spirit has come into being because of the flesh, it is a

wonder of wonders. Yet I marvel how this great wealth has appeared in this poverty.

30. Jesus said: Where there are three gods, they are gods. Where there are two or one, I am with him.

31. Jesus said: No prophet is accepted in his own village. A doctor does not heal those who know him.

32. Jesus said: A city built and fortified upon a high mountain cannot fall, nor can it remain hidden.

33. Jesus said: What you hear in your ear, proclaim from your rooftops.* For no man lights a lamp and sets it under a bushel nor puts it under a bushel nor puts it in a hidden place. No, he sets it on a stand so that all who come and go will see its light.

* There is an obscure, unimportant addition here.

34. Jesus said: If one blind man leads another, they will both fall into a ditch.

35. Jesus said: No one can enter a strong man's house and take it by force without tying his hands. Then he can plunder his house.

36. Jesus said: Do not worry from morning to evening or evening to morning about what you are going to put on.

37. His disciples said: When will you be revealed to us, and when will we see you? Jesus said: When you take off your clothes without shame and place them beneath your feet like little children and trample on them, then will you see the son of the living one without fear.

38. Jesus said: Often have you desired to hear these words that I am saying to you, and you have no one else from whom to hear them. The days will come when

you will seek me and not find me.

39. Jesus said: The Pharisees and the Scribes have received the keys of knowledge and hidden them. They have not entered nor permitted those to do so who desired to. But as for you, be wise as serpents and innocent as doves.

40. Jesus said: A vine has been planted away from the father. But as it has not strengthened, it will be pulled up by its roots and be destroyed.

41. Jesus said: He who has something in his hand will be given more. And he who has not will be deprived even of the little that he has.

42. Jesus said: Be passers-by.

43. His disciples said to him: Who are you to say these things to us? Jesus answered: You do not recognize who I am from what I say to you. No, you have become like the Jews. For they love the tree and hate its fruit, or they love the fruit and hate the tree.

44. Jesus said: He who blasphemes against the father will be forgiven. And he who blasphemes against the son will be forgiven. But he who blasphemes against the holy spirit will not be forgiven, neither on earth nor in heaven.

45. Jesus said: They do not gather grapes from thorns nor figs from thistles, for they yield no fruit. A good man brings forth good from his storehouse. A bad man brings forth evil from the evil storehouse in his heart and says evil things. For out of his heart's abundance he brings forth evil.

46. Jesus said: From Adam to John the Baptist none born of women is greater than John the Baptist so that he should not avert his gaze. But I have said that

whoever among you becomes as a child will know the kingdom and be greater than John.

47. Jesus said: A man cannot ride two horses nor draw two bows. A servant cannot serve two masters or he will honour one and disrespect the other. A man does not drink matured wine and immediately desire to drink the new. Nor is new wine poured into old skins for fear they burst. Nor is matured wine poured into new skins for fear it spoil. An old patch is not sewn on to a new garment for it would tear.

48. Jesus said: If two make peace with one another in this one house, they will say to the mountain, Move, and it will move.

49. Jesus said: Blessed are the solitary and the chosen, for you will find the kingdom. For you came from it and you will return to it again.

50. Jesus said: If they say to you, where have you come from? Tell them, We have come from the light, from where light came into being by itself. It came and showed itself in their image. If they say to you, Is it you? Answer, We are his sons, the chosen ones of the living father. If they ask you, What is the sign of your father in you? Answer, It is movement, and repose.

51. His disciples said to him: When will the rest of the dead happen, and when will the new world come? He said to them: What you are waiting for has come, but you do not know it.

52. His disciples said to him: Twenty-four prophets spoke in Israel, and they all spoke of you. He said to them: You have disregarded the one who is alive before you and have spoken of the dead.

53. His disciples said to him: Is circumcision of benefit or not?

He said to them: If it were of benefit, fathers would beget their children from their mothers circumcised. But the true circumcision in spirit has become wholly profitable.

54. Jesus said: Blessed are the poor for yours is the kingdom of heaven.

55. Jesus said: Whoever does not hate his father and his mother cannot be my disciple, and whoever does not hate his brothers and his sisters and take up his cross as I do will not be worthy of me.

56. Jesus said: He who has known the world has found a corpse and he who has found a corpse, the world is not worthy of him.

57. Jesus said: The father's kingdom is like a man who had good seed. His enemy came by night and sowed a weed among the good seed. The man did not let them pull out the weed. He said to them: No, in case you pull out the weed and the wheat with it. For on the day of the harvest the weeds will be easy to see and will be pulled out and burned.

58. Jesus said: Blessed is the man who has laboured. He has found life.

59. Jesus said: Look on the living one as long as you live, in case you die and try to see him and cannot.

60. They saw a Samaritan carrying a lamb on his way to Judaea. He said to his disciples: Why does he carry the lamb? They said to him: So that he may kill it and eat it. He said to them: While it is alive he will not eat it, but only if he kills it and it becomes a corpse. They said: Otherwise he will be unable to. He said to them: You also, seek for yourselves a place for rest, or

you may become a corpse and be eaten.

61. Jesus said: Two will rest upon a couch. One will die, the other live. Salome said: Who are you, man? You have climbed onto my couch and eaten from my table, as if you have come from someone. Jesus said to her: I am the one who comes from what is whole. To me it was given out of the things of my father. Salome said: I am your disciple. Jesus said: Therefore I say, when one is whole one will be filled with light, but when one is divided, one will be filled with darkness.

62. Jesus said: I reveal my mysteries to those worthy of my mysteries. What your right hand does, let not your left hand know.

63. Jesus said: There was a rich man possessed of much money. He said: I will use my money so that I may sow, reap and plant,

and I will fill my storehouses with fruit that I may want for nothing. These were his thoughts in his heart. And that night he died. Who has ears, let him hear.

64. Jesus said: A man was receiving guests. And when he had prepared the dinner he sent his servant to invite the guests. He went to the first and said to him, My master invites you. He answered, Some money of mine is in the hands of some merchants. They are coming to me this evening. I will go and give them their orders. I beg to be excused from the dinner.

He went to another and said to him, My master invites you. He answered, I have bought a house and they require a day's attendance from me. I shall not have time.

He went to another and said to him, My master invites you. He answered him, My friend is going to be married, and I am to organize the dinner. I am unable to come. I beg to be excused from the dinner.

He went to another and said to him, My master invites you. He answered, I have bought a village and I am going to collect the rent. I shall be unable to come. I beg to be excused.

He went and said to his master, Those that you invited to the dinner have begged to be excused. The master answered his servant, Go out on to the roads, and bring back anyone you find to have dinner. Neither buyers nor merchants will enter the places of my father.

65. He said: A . . . man had a vineyard. He gave it to husbandmen that they might work it and he collect its produce from them. He sent his servant so that the husbandmen might give him the produce of the vineyard. They seized his servant, they beat him and almost killed him. The servant came and told his master. His master said,

Perhaps they did not know him. He sent another servant, and the husbandmen beat him also. Then the master sent his son. He said, Perhaps they will respect my son. Those husbandmen, knowing he was heir to the vineyard, seized him and killed him. He who has ears, let him hear.

66. Jesus said: Show me the stone that the builders rejected. It is the cornerstone.

67. Jesus said: He who knows all but is lacking in himself is altogether lacking.

68. Jesus said: Blessed are you when they hate you and persecute you and find no place, wherever you have been persecuted.

69. Jesus said: Blessed are those who have been persecuted in their hearts. They are those who have truly known the father. Blessed are those who hunger

that the stomach of him who wishes it may be filled.

70. Jesus said: When you bring forth what is inside you, what you have will save you. When you do not have that inside you, what you do not have will kill you.

71. Jesus said: I shall destroy this house, and no one will be able to build it again.

72. A man said to him: Speak to my brothers that they may divide my father's possessions with me. He answered him: Man, who made me a divider? He turned to his disciples and said to them: I am not a divider, am I?

73. Jesus said: The harvest is indeed great but the workers are few. But beg the master that he send out workers to the harvest.

74. He said: Master, there are many around the well, but no one in the well.

75. Jesus said: There are many standing at the door, but it is the solitary that will enter the bridal chamber.

76. Jesus said: The kingdom of the father is like a merchant who had a load of merchandize and found a pearl. That merchant was wise. He sold the load and bought for himself the single pearl. You also, seek for his treasure that does not cease but endures, where no moth arrives to devour nor worm destroys.

77. Jesus said: I am the light that is over everything. I am everything. Everything has come forth from me, and everything has reached up to me. Split a piece of wood. I am there. Raise up the stone, and you will find me there.

78. Jesus said: Why did you come out into the field? To see a reed shaken by the wind? And to see a man dressed in soft

clothing? . . . your kings and potentates are dressed in soft clothing, and they will not be able to know the truth.

79. A woman in the crowd said to him: Blessed is the womb that bore you and the breasts that nourished you. He said to her: Blessed are those who have heard the word of the father and have truly kept it. For there will be a time when you will say, Blessed is the womb that has not conceived, and the breasts that have not given milk.

80. Jesus said: He who has known the world has found the body, and of him who has found the body the world is not worthy.

81. Jesus said: Let him who has become rich become king, and let him who has power put it away.

82. Jesus said: He who is near me is near the fire, and he who is far from me is far from the kingdom.

83. Jesus said: Images are manifest to a man, and the light within them is concealed in the image of the light of the father. He will be revealed, but his image is concealed by his light.

84. Jesus said: When you see your likeness, you are glad. But when you see your images that came into being before you, and that do not die nor become manifest, how much can you bear?

85. Jesus said: Adam came into being from great power and wealth, but he was not worthy of you. For if he had been worthy, he would not have tasted death.

86. Jesus said: Foxes have their holes and birds have their nests, but the son of man has nowhere to lay his head, and rest.

87. Jesus said: Wretched is the body that depends on a body, and wretched the soul that depends on these two.

88. Jesus said: The angels and the prophets will come to you and give you what is yours. And you also, give them what you have, and say to yourselves, When are they coming to take what is theirs?

89. Jesus said: Why do you wash the outside of the cup? Do you not see that he who made the inside is also he who made the outside?

90. Jesus said: Come to me, for my yoke is easy and my lordship gentle, and you will find rest for yourselves.

91. They said to him: Tell us who you are that we may believe in you. He said to them: You study the face of heaven and earth. But you do not recognize him who is before you. Nor do you know how to study this moment.

92. Jesus said: Seek and you will find. In those days the things you asked me about I did not tell you. Now I am willing to tell them, but you do not seek them.

93. Jesus said: Do not give what is holy to dogs in case they throw them on the dung heap. Do not throw pearls before swine in case they . . .

94. Jesus said: He who seeks will find, and to him who knocks it will be opened.

95. Jesus said: If you have money, do not lend it at interest. But give it to him who will not return it to you.

96. Jesus said: The father's kingdom is like a woman who took a little yeast and hid it in dough and made large loaves from it. He who has ears, let him hear.

97. Jesus said: The father's kingdom is like a woman carrying a jar filled with meal on a long walk. The handle of the jar broke and the meal spilled behind her on the road. She failed to notice her loss. When she reached her home, she put down the jar and found it empty.

98. Jesus said: The father's kingdom is like a man who wanted to kill someone powerful. At home he drew his sword and drove it into the wall to find out the strength of his hand. Then he killed the powerful man.

99. The disciples said to him: Your brothers and your mother are standing outside. He answered them: Those here who fulfil the will of my father are my brothers and my mother. It is they who will enter my father's kingdom.

100. They showed Jesus a gold coin and said to him: Caesar's men demand tribute from us. He answered them: Give to Caesar the things that are Caesar's, give to God the things that are God's, and give to me what is mine.

101. Jesus said: He who does not hate his father and his mother as I do cannot be a disciple of mine. And he who does not love his father and his mother as I do cannot be a disciple of mine. For my mother . . . but my true mother gave me life.

102. Jesus said: Woe to them, the Pharisees. For they are like a dog sleeping in the cattle manger. It neither eats nor lets the cattle eat.

103. Jesus said: Blessed is he who knows to what part the robbers are coming, so that he may get up, gather his . . . and arm himself before they arrive.

104. They said to Jesus: Come, let us pray today and fast. Jesus

answered: Then what sin have I committed or how have I been worsted? But when the bridegroom leaves the bridal chamber, that is the time that they should fast and pray.

105. Jesus said: He who knows father and mother will be called the son of a prostitute.

106. Jesus said: When you make the two into one, you will become sons of man. And when you say, Mountain, move, it will be moved.

107. Jesus said: The kingdom is like a shepherd who had a hundred sheep. The largest of them wandered off. He left the ninety-nine and searched after the one till he had found it. After this effort he said to the sheep, I love you more than the ninety-nine.

108. Jesus said: He who drinks from my mouth will become like me. I myself shall become that person, and the hidden things will be revealed to him.

109. Jesus said: The kingdom is like a man who had in his field a hidden treasure of which he was unaware. And after his death he left it to his son. The son was also unaware, and, after taking possession of the field, he sold it. The purchaser came and ploughed it and found the treasure. He began to lend money at interest to anyone he chose.

110. Jesus said: Let the man who has found the world and become rich renounce the world.

111. Jesus said: The heavens and the earth will be rolled up before you. And he who is living in the living one will not see death. For Jesus says: Of him who finds himself, the world is not worthy.

112. Jesus said: Woe to the flesh that depends on the soul. Woe to the soul that depends on the flesh.

113. His disciples said to him: When will the kingdom come? Jesus said: It does not come by one's looking for it. They will not say, Look, here! or, Look, there! But the father's kingdom is spread out over the earth, and people fail to see it.

114. Simon Peter said to them: Let Mary leave us, for women are not worthy of the life. Jesus said: Look, I shall lead her, so as to bring her to maleness, that she also may become a living spirit like you males. For every woman who makes herself male will enter the kingdom of heaven.

VIII

THE SECRET GOSPEL
OF MARK

No event could be more startling in the progress of our understanding of Jesus and his teachings than the rediscovery of a second and more complete gospel by the earliest of the evangelists. But one problem cannot be ignored: did it ever actually exist?

In 1958 Dr Morton Smith, an American scholar, was invited to return to the monastery of Mar Saba – situated in the desert twelve miles outside Jerusalem – where he had stayed for a few weeks during the Second World War. His task was to study and catalogue its manuscripts.

In the course of his research, while inspecting a seventeenth-century edition of Ignatius of Antioch, he discovered some tiny eighteenth-century handwriting in Greek on the endpaper. Carefully transcribed, this text revealed itself as part of a letter written by the Christian writer Clement of Alexandria, about the year AD 200, to an unknown Theodore. The content was sensational. Clement was endeavouring to reassure Theodore about a

From the Letters of the Most Holy Clement, Author of the Stromateis, to Theodoros:

You did well to muzzle the secret teachings of the Carpocratians; for these are men prophesied as being wandering stars; they are wandering from the narrow road of commands to the limitless abyss of the flesh and physical sin. For, having become puffed up with pride, as they say, 'with the matters of Satan', they are unaware that they are throwing themselves out into the gloom of the darkness of a lie. And although they are boasting that they are free, they have become servants of slavish lusts; so then, they must be resisted in every way and altogether – because even if they would speak something true, not even would the lover of the truth agree with them. For neither are all 'true things' the truth, nor should something that seems to be true according to human notions be preferred to the true truth that is according to faith.

Now then, concerning the common chatter about the divine inspired gospel according to Mark, while some things are complete lies, others, even if they embrace some true matters, are not then communicated truthfully; for true matters blended together with fictions become false currency, just as it is said that 'even the salt is made tasteless'. At any rate, Mark, during the time Peter spent in Rome, wrote about the deeds of the Lord, not, however, reporting all of them, nor indeed hinting at the secret ones, but he picked out those he knew were most useful for the growth of those being instructed in the faith. After Peter was martyred, Mark moved on to Alexandria and carried treatises of his own and of Peter, from which he transferred into his first book those things appropriate for those progressing in knowledge and he arranged a more spiritual gospel document which he had been introduced to by the Carpocratians, a heretical sect who believed *inter alia* that Jesus had normal human parents. And in view of the falsifications that the Carpocratians had been guilty of, Clement thought fit to tell Theodore in some detail about a gospel of which no other knowledge survives.

Mark, said Clement, had gone to Alexandria after Peter's death, taking his own notes and those of Peter, which he had used to amplify his earlier gospel to create a more spiritual gospel for initiates. On his death he had left this advanced gospel to the Alexandrian church, where it was still carefully guarded and knowledge of it released only to a select few.

Nevertheless, Carpocrates had acquired a copy, which he had proceeded to corrupt. Clement therefore would now enlighten Theodore where misunderstanding had arisen.

He continues by quoting two passages at length which belong to Chapter Ten of our standard version of Mark. One of these covers the raising of Lazarus; and the second relates to an incident in Jericho.

The first and more important of these episodes reveals that, a few days after Lazarus was returned to life, Jesus involved him in a nocturnal excursion, by which he was taught the mystery of the kingdom of heaven. Clement is at pains to stress that this text does not include 'naked one with naked one'.[1]

for use by those who have been perfected. Even so, he did not indiscreetly reveal these secrets, nor did he write down the hierophantic lesson of the Lord. Instead, adding other things as well to the deeds written previously, he still made further inclusions of certain teachings, the interpretation of which he knew would initiate those listening into the mysteries of the inner sanctum of the truth that has been covered seven times. In this way, as I see it, he made preparations, not grudgingly nor without precautions, and dying, he left behind his writing in Alexandria, where it is still now kept securely, being read only to those initiated into the great mysteries. But since abominable demons devise ruin for the race of men, Carpocrates, taught by these men and using deceitful skills, enslaved one elder of the church in Alexandria, with the result that he carried off from him a copy of the secret gospel.

And he interpreted it according to his blasphemous and fleshly vision, but yet even tainted the undefiled and holy teachings, mixing in the most shameless lies. It is from this mixture that the dogma of the Carpocratians is drained off. So, as I have said before, one must never give way to these men; one must not concede to them, when they propose falsified things, that the secret gospel is by Mark, but it must be denied with an oath. For all true things must not be spoken to every person; because of this the wisdom of God recommends through Solomon 'Answer a fool from his folly', teaching that the light of truth must be hidden away from those who are mentally blind. For example, they say 'it will be taken away from one not understanding' and 'let the fool walk in darkness', but we are sons of light, enlightened by the rising from the crown of the spirit of the lord; it is said of the spirit of the lord that 'there

Dr Smith observed that at the same chronological position in John's gospel the Lazarus episode could be found; and he also considered there to be sound evidence that Mark's was the more primitive version.

Scholars have not been inclined to view all this as an elaborate hoax.[2] The second passage, for instance, explains the awkward verse 46 – 'They reached Jericho; and as they left Jericho . . .' – coming between the arrival and departure.[3]

And what of 14.41–42? '. . . *Sleep on now* and *take your rest*: it is enough, the hour is come, behold the son of man is betrayed into the hands of sinners. *Rise up* and let us go . . .'[4] Mark's gospel may be much more explicable by reference to a number of missing sections, so that one may venture to suggest the Secret Gospel actually *preceded* our orthodox version and should be viewed as the original gospel.[5]

But, for lack of any further text, we are reduced to hypotheses, and the awareness that early Christianity may have involved higher secrets perhaps forever lost. Since Clement of Alexandria knew this text, perhaps there are other clues still to be discovered in his writings.

For instance, one might consider his comments on *gnosis* (knowledge) in the Miscellanies, quoted by T. Churton in his book *The Gnostics*: '. . . and this latter [i.e. *gnosis*], as it passes on into love, begins at once to establish a mutual friendship between that which knows and that which is known. And perhaps he who has arrived at this stage has is freedom', for all things are pure to the pure; now then, I will not hesitate to answer for you the things asked. I will speak refuting the falsehoods with the very matters of the gospel; after 'They were on the road going up to Jerusalem', and from there until 'the third day he will arise', it adds here, as the phrase goes:

'And they came to Bethany, and there was there one woman whose brother had died: and going up she bowed to Jesus and said to him "Son of David, pity me!" but the disciples criticized her, and having become angry, Jesus went away with her to the garden where the tomb was and immediately there was a great sound from the tomb and having approached, Jesus rolled away the stone from the door of the tomb and immediately coming in where the young man was, he reached out a hand and woke him. Seizing the hand, the young man looked at him, loved him and began to entreat him that he might go with him, and having left the tomb they went to the home of the young man, for he was rich. And after six days he gave him orders, and when evening arrived, the youth comes to him, having put on linen over his naked body. And he remained with him that night, for Jesus taught him the mystery of the Kingdom of God. Standing up from there, he returned the other side of the Jordan.'

Then these matters are followed by: 'And James and John approached him,' and the whole passage, but the 'naked one with naked one' and the other things which you wrote about are not found. After 'And he came to Jericho' it only brings in:

'And they were there, the sister of the young man whom Jesus loved and his mother and Salome; and Jesus did not receive them.'[6]

But the many other things which you wrote both seem and are lies. So then the true already attained equality with the angels. At any rate, after he has reached the final ascent in the flesh, he still continues to advance, as is fit, and presses on through the holy Hebdomad into the Father's house, to that which is indeed the Lord's abode, being destined there to be, as it were, a light standing and abiding forever, absolutely secure from all vicissitude.'

interpretation and according to the true philosophy . . .

A reconstruction of that portion of the Secret Gospel recorded in Clement's letter:

1. Mark 10.32–35 with addition. And they were on the road going up to Jerusalem. And Jesus went before them, and they were astonished and followed fearfully. And he took the twelve again and began to tell them the things that were going to happen to him, saying, Behold we go up to Jerusalem and the son of man will be delivered to the chief priests and the scribes, and they will condemn him to death, and deliver him to the gentiles; and they will mock him and whip him and spit on him and kill him, and the third day he will arise.

['And they came to Bethany, and there was there one woman whose brother had died: and going up she bowed to Jesus and said to him "Son of David, pity me!" but the disciples criticized her, and having become angry, Jesus went away with her to the garden where the tomb was and immediately there was a great sound from the tomb, and having approached, Jesus rolled away the stone from the door of the tomb; and immediately coming in where the young man was, he reached out a hand and woke him. Seizing the hand, the young man looked at him, loved him and began to entreat him that he might go with him, and having left the tomb they went to the home of the young man, for he was rich. And after six days he gave him orders, and when evening arrived, the youth comes to him, having put on linen over his naked body. And he remained with him that night, for Jesus taught him the mystery of the Kingdom of God. Standing up from there, he returned to the other side of the Jordan.']

And James and John the sons of Zebedee approached him . . . *

*Clement omits 'the sons of Zebedee'.

2. Mark 10.46 with addition – And they* came to Jericho.

[And they were there, the sister of the young man whom Jesus loved and his mother and Salome, and Jesus did not receive them.] And as he went out of Jericho with his disciples . . .

*Clement writes 'he', not 'they'.

IX

MISCELLANEOUS
SAYINGS OF JESUS

Scattered through the writings of the early church fathers are sundry statements attributed to Jesus, in many cases bearing the hallmarks of apparent authenticity. But the essential problem with alleged quotation is that – quite apart from accidental or intended misquotation – it falls into one of three categories. First, the spirit or meaning of the original utterance; second, the approximate form of the words; third, the exact form of the words.

Many people have put together collections of Jesus' sayings that they believed belong to the third grouping. But the task of distinguishing these from the others is next to impossible.

1. The expression, 'Be astute money-changers!' is well attested by Clement of Alexandria, Epiphanius and others. M. R. James takes Paul's words: 'Prove all things, hold fast that which is good' as a comment on it. Was it said as part of a discourse after Jesus threw the money-changers out of the Temple?[1]

2. 'There shall be divisions and conflicts' is quoted by Justin and other later sources. It may invite comparison with the sixteenth saying of the Gospel of Thomas and is a warning of false prophets to come.

3. Clement of Alexandria and Origen both quote, Origen more completely, 'For ask', he said, 'for the great things, and the small things will be offered to you.' Clement links it with Matthew 6.33, of which it is possibly a paraphrase and adds: 'Ask for the heavenly things and the earthly will be offered to you.'

4. 'For he proclaimed to us when he was teaching, that what is weak will be saved through what is strong.'

5. For the saying had gone before that 'No one who has not been tempted will reach the heavenly kingdom'.[2]

Tertullian, one of several writers who quote this, gives this a Gethsemane context, saying, 'The disciples were tempted because they fell asleep, so that they forsook the Lord when he was taken . . .'

This is really a negative or mirror variation of the Epistle of James 1.12: Blessed is the man that endures temptation, for when he is tried he will receive the crown of life, which the Lord has promised to those that love him. (The reader may care to consider the saying in the light of Jesus' request in the Lord's Prayer.)

6. The fourth-century writer, Ephraem of Syria, cites the

following in his commentary on the raising of Lazarus and Jesus' distress at the tomb: But that he was distressed agrees with what he said, 'How long shall I be with you and speak with you?' And in another place, 'I am weary of this generation. They proved me . . . ten times, but these twenty times and ten times ten times.'[3]

7. The following quotation comes from the Clementine Homilies, but other writers also provide evidence for it. Clement of Alexandria speaks of it as taken from 'a certain gospel'. Is it possible that this is Mark's secret gospel?

We remember our Lord and teacher, when giving commands he said to us, 'Guard the mysteries for me and the sons of my house.'

This is referred to[4] in Mark 4.11 with the meaning that 'the principle of spiritual selection is always at work'.

8. Because of this the Saviour says, 'Be saved, you and your soul.'

9. The Lord said: 'Even if you are settled by my breast and do not carry out my orders, I will reject you, saying, "Withdraw from me, I do not know where you are from, you workers of lawlessness."' It is a variant of a text at Matthew 7.23, also to be found more closely matching in the Gospel of the Nazareans. This is conspicuously the fierce utterance of a kind man.

'New' quotations appear in every period and are virtually numberless. The following, quoted in Latin out of a twelfth-century Old English sermon, may be from some lost source such as Papias: 'Be you brave, and fight with the old serpent, and you shall receive an everlasting kingdom.' But the language is certainly not typical of the gospels. The old serpent is

86

referred to twice in the Book of Revelation (12.9 and 20.2).

The famous saying inscribed on a mosque in Fathpur-Sikri in India and known from at least the eighth century in Islamic literature cannot be omitted here: Jesus, on whom be peace, has said: 'The world is a bridge. Go over it, but do not install yourselves upon it.'[5] The interest in this saying cannot be lessened by the recent rediscovery of the Gospel of Thomas, in which Saying 42 reads: 'Be passers-by.'

Lastly, I shall include the charming Islamic tale of the carcase of the dead dog lying in 'Nazareth's narrow street' and tainting the atmosphere. 'Then . . . there came Isa, the son of Mary, of great fame for mighty deeds performed in Allah's name. He said, "How lovely are its teeth, so sharp, and white as pearls": then went his way.'[6] This story was famous long before the twelfth century when a Persian wrote a poem on it.

X

CLEMENT OF ROME'S
SAYINGS OF JESUS

The particular interest in Clement's First Epistle lies in its being the earliest datable Christian document outside the New Testament canon. Addressed to the Corinthians from Rome, it has been dated to *c.* AD 96, the author being Bishop of Rome at the time. Very little is known about him. Possible identifications with the Clement mentioned by Paul as his fellow-labourer (Phil. IV.3) and with the consul of AD 95, Titus Flavius Clemens, a nobleman, are not thought likely. However, a later historian informs us[1] that the consul was executed by Domitian for his 'atheism' – a term often used for Christianity – so that the bishop may well have come from the consul's family if not actually being the consul. It has also been suggested that he could have been a freedman of the consul.

The letter – discovered[2] in a Greek Bible manuscript presented to Charles I in 1628 – was written to settle disputes that had arisen in the Corinthian church and opens with what would seem to be a reference to the recent

1. ... Especially remembering the words of the Lord Jesus, which he uttered, to teach kindness and forbearance; for he spoke as follows:

'Show mercy; that you may receive mercy; forgive that you may be forgiven; as you do, so shall it be done to you; as you give, so shall it be given to you; as you judge, so shall you be judged; as you show kindness, so shall kindness be shown to you; with what scales you measure, it shall be measured to you likewise.'[3]

2. Remember the words of Jesus our lord. For he said, 'Woe to that man: it would have been better for him if he had not been born than to offend one of my chosen; it would have been better for him to have had a millstone hung around his neck and been cast into the sea than to lead one of my chosen astray.' (Compare Luke 17.2.)

persecution under Domitian. Its status was so high that it was virtually classed with the canonical documents in the earliest Christian era.

Nevertheless, Clement uses quotation in what is often a very casual manner, combining different texts from memory, and sometimes perhaps invoking the spirit without reference to the exact words of the original. The accompanying two quotations give the appearance of being derived from lost sources. That is all one can really say – beyond that, they must command the highest interest as belonging to the period when the gospels were written.

XI

QUADRATUS

The continuing presence of those Jesus healed

All that we know with confidence about Quadratus is derived from Eusebius, and the one surviving fragment of his writing that Eusebius has preserved for us. In the reign of the emperor Hadrian (AD 117–38), Quadratus mounted a reasoned defence of the Christian religion to him – the first of a number of 'Apologies' by Christian authors.[1] Eusebius says he was intelligent and, in his beliefs, orthodox, and that his book was written as a response to some troublemakers, with unknown results. He may be the same as a Bishop of Athens of that name (where Hadrian wintered in 125–6, and 129–30). But perhaps he resided in Asia. He was famous for the gift of prophecy.

The interest of the fragment lies in the recognition that there were not necessarily only Christian witnesses to Jesus' ministry. Some of those Jesus healed – whether Christian or otherwise – survived as living proof of his miraculous powers, perhaps even beyond the end of the first century. And one would guess, though the text is not quite clear, that Quadratus had met some of them personally, and perhaps heard their stories.

The works of the Saviour have been with us always, for they were genuine. Those who were healed or raised from the dead not only appeared as healed and raised but were also constantly present, not only when the Saviour was amongst us but also after he had departed, so that some of them have lived right up to our own time.[2]

XII

PAPIAS

Jesus' vision of the coming kingdom, and Judas Iscariot's disenchantment

Papias, Bishop of Hierapolis, a city of Phrygia in what is now western Turkey, belongs to the latter half of the first century and the beginning of the second. In his younger days, he tells us in the preface to his work (five books entitled *An Exposition of the Lord's Sayings*), he carefully enquired about the sayings of the apostles from those who had heard them as well as for 'what Aristion and the elder John . . . were (still) saying', and expresses his preference for a 'living and abiding voice' over things to be found in books.[1]

The great church historian Eusebius speaks of him dismissively as a man of very small intelligence but does not support this statement with any hard evidence. It is surprising, however, that Papias should bother his readers with a distasteful piece of Jewish folklore about Judas Iscariot's being taken down alive after an attempt at suicide by hanging and contracting a loathsome disease thereafter to become 'a great example of impiety'. And still more

As the elders who saw John the Lord's disciple remembered hearing from him how the Lord would teach about those times and say:

'The time will come when vines come forth, each bearing ten thousand boughs, and ten thousand branches on a single bough; yes, and on a single branch ten thousand shoots, and on every shoot ten thousand clusters, and in every cluster ten thousand grapes; and every grape once pressed will provide twenty-five measures of wine. And when one of those saints seizes a cluster, another cluster will cry, "I am better, take me, bless the Lord through me." Likewise also a grain of wheat will produce ten thousand heads, and each head will have ten thousand grains, and each grain will produce ten pounds of faultless, finest flour. And the other fruit and seeds and vegetation will produce in corresponding proportions. And all the animals eating that food taken from the earth will become at peace with one another and in harmony, and entirely submissive to humans.'

And he added:

'Believers can believe these things, and when Judas ... the betrayer disbelieved and asked, How then will the Lord bring about such produce? The Lord answered, "Those will see who arrive at those times." '[2]

surprising is the description, which he derives from John, of the coming kingdom of Jesus that he says will exist in a physical sense.

Eusebius records from him interesting statements on the formation of the gospels of Matthew and Mark and also tells us that Papias included in his work 'some strange parables of the saviour, and teachings'. One story of Papias' that receives specific mention is of a woman wrongly accused of many sins before the Lord. This story, also to be found according to Eusebius in the Gospel of the Hebrews, is of particular interest, since it is possible to equate it with a story in the seventh chapter of John's gospel, where the story is considered an interpolation.

Papias' work survives only as fragments quoted by later authors. But interestingly there seems to have been a copy in France at Nîmes in the thirteenth century, and another in England as late as the fifteenth, so that just possibly the full text may still turn up. Few early Christian texts would be more eagerly desired.

In the accompanying extract, Papias' description of the coming kingdom is the more intriguing for the response of Judas Iscariot. Do we have here a partial explanation for Judas' conduct?

XIII

HEGESIPPUS

The murder of Jesus' brother; Vespasian's search for the family of David; Jesus' great-nephews' meeting with Domitian

This second-century author, a much-travelled Christian known to have visited Corinth and Rome, gathered traditions of the early church, pursuing Christian beliefs and collecting historical details of earliest Christianity which he incorporated into five books. Eusebius records his use of the Gospel of the Hebrews and an uncertain Syriac Gospel.[1] He also provides a number of extracts – all that remains of Hegesippus' writing.

Hegesippus' long account of the life and death of James, Jesus' brother, is our main account of James outside the New Testament, stressing his importance[2] after Jesus' death, and his holiness. After his death *c.* AD 62 and the terrible events at Rome in AD 64 (see Tacitus), the next known general persecution – applying to orthodox Jews and Jewish Christians alike – was instigated by the emperor Vespasian, who was determined that, after the fall of Jerusalem in

Extract 1:

The care of the church passed to James the brother of the Lord, and to the apostles. He was called the 'Just' by all men from the Lord's time to our own; for there were many with the name of James, but he had been holy from his mother's womb. He drank no wine or strong drink, nor did he eat meat. No razor passed over his head, he never anointed himself with oil, nor did he go to the baths. He was the only person allowed to enter the sanctuary, for he did not wear wool but linen. He used to go into the temple alone and be found kneeling and praying for forgiveness for the people, so that his knees became hard like a camel's through his constant kneeling, worshipping God and asking for forgiveness for the people. Because of his great righteousness he was called Just and Oblias [which is Hebrew for 'Defence of the People' and 'Justice'], as the prophets say of him. Anyway,

some of the seven sects among the people, which I have already described in my commentaries, asked him what was the 'Gate of Jesus'. He replied that it was the Saviour. Some were led by this to believe that Jesus was the Christ. The sects mentioned above did not believe in resurrection nor in someone coming to give judgement to each man according to his deeds. But those who did believe, believed because of James. Now since many of the government were believers, there was uproar amongst the Jews, with the scribes and Pharisees saying that there was a danger of the whole people expecting Jesus as the Christ. So they got together and spoke to James. 'We appeal to you,' they said, 'to restrain the mob, since they have got the wrong idea about Jesus and think he is the Christ. We appeal to you to persuade everyone who comes for the day of the Passover about Jesus – for we all obey you. We and the

99

AD 70, the royal dynasty of David should not trouble the Romans in the future (Extract 2).

In this policy of rooting out the family he was followed by his cruel second son, Domitian, who actually demanded that Jesus' great-nephews be brought before him, only to conclude the interview peacefully when he saw they represented no threat (Extract 3).

Hegesippus believed this event put an end to a short-lived persecution,[3] which also seems to have led to John's exile on the island of Patmos. Others who suffered may have included the serving consul Flavius Clemens (executed) and his wife Flavia Domitilla (exiled). It is interesting to note again the status enjoyed by the Desposunoi – the Lord's people, who, once thrust into the limelight, were thereafter accorded high status within the Christian community.

whole people bear witness that you are just and no respecter of persons. So persuade the mob not to get the wrong idea about Jesus. For the whole people and all of us obey you. Stand on the battlements of the temple, so that you can be seen from below, and let your words be heard by all the people. Because of the Passover all the tribes have gathered, and the Gentiles too.' So the above-mentioned scribes and Pharisees stood James on the battlements of the temple and shouted up to him, 'Hey, Just one, we all owe obedience to you. Since the people are straying after Jesus who was crucified, tell us this: what is the Gate of Jesus?' And James answered in a loud voice, 'Why are you asking me about the Son of Man? He is sitting in heaven at the right hand of the Great Power, and he will come on the clouds of heaven.' And many people were convinced and gloried in James' testimony, saying 'Hosanna to the son of David.' Then the same scribes and Pharisees said to each other, 'We were fools to give Jesus this publicity. Let us go up and throw him down, so that they get scared and stop believing him.' Then they shouted, 'Oh, oh, even the Just one is in error!' And they fulfilled the words of Isaiah 'Let us remove the just man since he is inconvenient to us. Yet they shall eat the fruit of their works.' They went up and cast down the Just one, and said to one another, 'Let us stone James the Just.' They began to stone him – for when he fell he had not been killed. But he turned and knelt, praying, 'O Lord Father, forgive them, for they know not what they do.' While they were stoning him, one of the priests of the sons of Rechab son of Rechabim, to whom the prophet Jeremiah bore witness, shouted, 'Stop! What are you doing? The Just one is praying for us.' Then one of them, a laundryman, took the club which he used to beat out clothes and struck James on the head. Thus he suffered martyrdom. They buried him in the place near the temple, and his tombstone still remains there by the temple. He became a true witness for the Jews and the Greeks, that Jesus is the Christ. Immediately afterwards Vespasian began to besiege them.

Extract 2:

And in addition to this Hegesippus says that after the capture of Jerusalem Vespasian ordered all those who were of the family of David to be sought out, so that no one of the royal house should be left amongst the Jews, and for this reason a great persecution was again inflicted on the Jews.

Extract 3:

There still survived from the family of the Lord grandsons of Judas,* who was said to be his

natural brother, whom they informed against as being of the family of David. The official brought them before the Emperor Domitian; for, just as Herod was, he was afraid of the coming of the Christ. When Domitian asked them if they were of the house of David, they said they were. Then he asked how much property they owned, and what their finances were: they said they possessed only nine thousand denarii, divided equally between them; but they did not have this in money but in the valuation of only twenty-five acres, on which they paid taxes and worked to support themselves. Then they showed their hands and the hardness of their bodies as proof of their labour, and the calluses which stood out on their hands as a result of their continual work. When they were asked about Christ and his kingdom, what it was like and where and when it would appear, they gave the answer that it was not of this world or earthly, but heavenly and angelic, and it would come at the end of Time, when he would come in glory to judge the living and the dead and reward every man according to his deeds. At this Domitian did not condemn them, but let them go, despising them as simple, and he decreed that the persecution of the church should stop. But when they were released they became leaders of the churches, as they had borne witness and were also of the Lord's family, and they remained alive in the peace which prevailed until Trajan.

* Named elsewhere as Zoker and James.

XIV

IRENAEUS

John flees a heretic

One last link between the age of the apostles and later times was the splendid Polycarp – of no outstanding intelligence, but unshakably firm in his beliefs – who had known John and perhaps other apostles in his youth and, having been appointed to Asia 'by the apostles' as Bishop of Smyrna (modern Izmir in Turkey), died a martyr's death in AD 155.

Irenaeus, his disciple,[1] became Bishop of Lyon (in modern-day France) towards the end of the century. His important work 'Against Heresies' is a mine of knowledge on the early church. He is supposed to have died in Severus' persecution of AD 202.

And there are some who heard him [Polycarp] tell how John the disciple of the Lord travelled to Ephesus to bathe, and seeing Cerinthus[2] inside he sprang out of the baths without having bathed, calling out, 'Let's get out of here, before the baths collapse! Cerinthus is in here, and an enemy of the truth.'

X V

CLEMENT
OF ALEXANDRIA

John confronts a robber in his
mountain hideout

Clement of Alexandria, born at Athens about AD 150, converted to Christianity and travelled abroad seeking instruction. A learned and wide-ranging philosopher, he was also a voluminous writer, and a number of his works still survive including the *Stromateis* or *Miscellanies*, a philosophical work incorporating a number of earlier texts. He died shortly after AD 210.

The following story relates to the end of John's life, after the death of the emperor Domitian in AD 96: he had returned from exile to his old home at Ephesus. He must have been well into his eighties, if Clement has placed this incident at the right point in his life – the last of the apostles and a revered figure. It might serve as a commentary on the parable of the good shepherd: 'Does he not leave the ninety-nine and go into the mountains and seek that which has gone astray?'

Listen to a story which is no legend but a true account concerning John the Apostle which has been handed down and preserved in memory.

On the death of the tyrant, John travelled from the island of Patmos to Ephesus. He used to go when invited to the neighbouring districts of the gentiles, in some cases to appoint bishops, in others to organize whole churches, and in others again to ordain one of those indicated by the Spirit. Anyway, he arrived in one of the cities nearby (some actually give its name)* and encouraged the brotherhood in various ways; then, in the presence of everyone, he looked at the man appointed and observed to him a young man strong in body, with an intelligent face and warm heart. 'I recommend this man to you,' he said, 'with the greatest enthusiasm, in the presence of the church, with Christ as my witness.' The bishop received him and made all promises, and John again addressed him and adjured him in the same words.

Then he went back to Ephesus and the bishop took the young man who had been entrusted to him into his house, fed him, brought him up, looked after him, and finally baptized him. Later he relaxed his excessive care and guardianship, since he had placed on him the seal of the Lord as the perfect safeguard. But the young man had gained his freedom too soon, and he fell in with some dissolute youths of evil habits, who corrupted him. To begin with they led him on with extravagant parties, then took him with them on their nocturnal robberies, then encouraged him to greater crimes. He gradually got used to this, and, like an unbroken powerful horse straying from the straight path and tearing at the

* Smyrna, and its bishop seemingly the very young Polycarp, or perhaps his predecessor if there was one.

At any rate, this delightful story is a precious instance of a fragment of apostolic biography to be found outside the canonical books.

bit, he rushed all the more into the abyss because of his natural energy. Finally he renounced salvation from God. Abandoning petty misdeeds, since he was ruined once and for all, he decided to carry out some major crime and to suffer the same fate as the rest. He took these same companions and formed a robber-band. He himself was a born gang-leader, the most violent, bloodthirsty and ruthless of them all.

Time passed, and when some necessity arose they summoned John. John dealt with the matters for which he had come, and then said, 'Well now, bishop, give me back the deposit which Christ and I left with you, witnessed by the church over which you preside.' First the bishop panicked, thinking he was being importuned for money which he had not received, and he could neither believe a charge about something he didn't have, nor could he disbelieve John. But

when the latter said, 'It's the young man I'm asking for, and the soul of our brother,' he gave a deep groan and even wept a little, saying 'He is dead.' 'How, and by what kind of death?' 'He has died to God,' the bishop replied. 'He turned out wicked and abandoned, and finally a brigand. And now instead of the church he has taken to the mountains with an armed band of men like himself.' The apostle rent his garments and beat his head with a great cry of grief. 'A fine guardian I left for the soul of our brother,' he said. 'But prepare a horse for me immediately and let me have a guide for the way.' He rode off just as he was, straight from the church. As soon as he got there he was captured by the robbers' lookout, but he did not try to run away nor did he beg for mercy, but shouted, 'This is what I've come for! Take me to your leader!' The leader was waiting for him, armed as he was, but when he recognized John, he was ashamed and ran away. John, forgetting his age, followed as fast as he could shouting, 'Why are you running away from me, my son? I am your father, unarmed and old! Have pity on me, my son, don't be afraid! You still have hope of life. I will intercede with Christ for you. If necessary, I will willingly suffer your death, just as the Lord suffered for us. I will give up my life to save yours. Stop. Trust me. Christ sent me.' Hearing this the young man stood with eyes downcast, then threw down his weapons and began to shake and weep bitterly. John came up to him and the young man embraced him, pleading for forgiveness as best he could with sobbing, being baptized a second time in his tears, only hiding his right hand. The old man gave his pledge and promised that he had obtained forgiveness from the Saviour, and praying he knelt down, kissing that same right hand as though it had now been purified by his repentance. Then he brought him back to the church. There he prayed with abundant prayers, joined him in the challenge of continual fasting, and enchanted his mind with various talk, and did not leave him, so they say, till he had restored him to the church, thus leaving a great example of true repentance, a great token of regeneration, and a trophy of resurrection for all to see.

XVI

JULIUS AFRICANUS

Jesus' relatives' pride in their family

This Christian philosopher, living towards the end of the second and beginning of the third centuries in Aelia Capitolina (the Roman city that had replaced Jerusalem) went on an embassy to the emperor Elagabalus, *c.* AD 220, and succeeded in obtaining for Emmaus city rank and the title of Nicopolis. His writings included works on chronography and a miscellany chiefly relating to magic. In a letter to an unidentified Aristides, he attempted to explain the discrepancies between the two genealogies of Jesus found in the gospels.

In the course of this letter he refers to a story put about by Jesus' relatives, 'whether to magnify their origin or simply to declare what actually happened'.

This story tells how Herod the Great's father, Antipater, had originally been carried off captive from a temple of Apollo in Palestine, where his father served in a lowly capacity, and had risen to success in the place of his captivity after his father could not pay his ransom.

And among these [i.e. the families who preserved their records] happen to be those already mentioned, called "the Lord's people" because of their link with the Saviour's family. These coming out of Nazareth and Cochaba,[1] villages in Judaea, to other parts of the country set forth the above-mentioned genealogy as accurately as they could . . .

The story is untrue, but it is interesting to see descendants of the House of David, long defunct as a political force, casting what seem like aspersions on the rival dynasty. The family pride is very evident.

The author continues by saying that Herod caused the public registers of Jewish families to be burned but was unable to prevent a few families from preserving their own records.

XVII

SAMUEL THE SMALL

The Jews curse the Christians

This first-century rabbi composed a prayer called the *Birkath haMinim* at Jamnia in the time of Gamaliel, *c.* AD 85. It is the twelfth of the eighteen Benedictions and a very ancient part of the synagogue service, surviving in variant forms. The term 'minim' may have originally meant Jewish Christian.

This prayer, for all its harshness, was intended as a test benediction to keep heretics out of the synagogue.

The attribution of this prayer to Samuel the Small rests upon this text: 'Rabbi Gamaliel said to the wise "Is there any man that knows how to prepare a prayer about the heretics?"[1] Samuel the Small stood up and prepared it.'[2]

For the apostates may there not be hope, and may the kingdom of insolence be speedily eradicated in our days, and may the Nazareans and the heretics be suddenly ruined, may they be wiped away from the book of lives and may they not be written with the just; blessed are you, God, who bring down the insolent.

XVIII

BARCOCHBA

A new Messiah? His hatred of the Christians

If the Romans thought the crushing of the courageous Jewish resistance to their authority and the destruction of Jerusalem in the first Jewish War (AD 66–70) was enough to control this people, they were mistaken. Simmering discontent led to disturbances at the end of Trajan's reign. And, in the time of his successor Hadrian, a serious rebellion broke out under Barcochba. This was ruthlessly put down by Julius Severus in AD 135, but not before Barcochba had apparently succeeded in reoccupying Jerusalem.[1] Hadrian was to rebuild it, adding the stipulation that no Jew should be allowed to enter it.

Eusebius records the rebel as a bloodthirsty brigand who acted as if he were God's gift ('a luminary descended from heaven') to his followers, and Justin the Apologist, Barcochba's contemporary, adds this: 'Barcochba . . . ordered that savage punishments should be inflicted on Christians alone, if they did not renounce Jesus as the Christ and blaspheme.'[2]

From Simeon ben Kosbah to Yeshua ben Galgolah and the men of the fortified place,[*] Greetings. I am calling the heavens as a witness upon me that if any man from the Galilleans [sic] that you saved will do harm,[**] I will place iron fetters on your feet, as I did to Ben Aflul. Simeon ben Kosbah, prince of Israel.

[*] Or, your association
[**] Or, that I saved is harmed.

This letter[3] of his found at Murabba'at near Jerusalem in 1952 can be interpreted in different ways. But, by reference to Justin's remark, it is just possible that the letter is warning an important lieutenant of the possible consequences of his milder treatment of Galilean Christians. But the problem here is that these Galileans are not necessarily Christians at all, though, if they are not, it is unclear why Barcochba should be expecting trouble from them. Interestingly, Galilee became a stronghold of Judaism for many years following the revolt.

XIX

TALMUD

Jesus' illegitimacy; an alternative account of his trial and execution; a first-century Christian healer

That great corpus of Jewish lore and law known as the Talmud is datable to *c.* AD 500 but is recognized as including much earlier material. The small number of early Christian references seems to reflect a relatively unrecorded period of Jewish history in the Talmud, the absence of the still earlier and vitally important figure of Judas Maccabaeus being a case in point.

In the first passage, we meet a rabbi's statement dating probably from the first half of the second century – a colleague of his was killed in Barcochba's rebellion. It appears to oppose the virgin birth of Jesus by indicating that a married woman (Mary) did not have her child by her husband.

In the second passage, it is interesting to see the Jews apparently lacking a sense of the *twelve* apostles. These five appear to include Matthew and Thaddaeus (sometimes equated

1. Rabbi Simeon Ben 'Azzai said 'I obtained a scroll of genealogical records in Jerusalem, and written on it was "A man, such-and-such is a bastard, being born from a woman with a husband."'

2. There were five pupils of Yeshu: Mattai, Naqai, Netser as well as Buni and Todah.*

3. On the eve of Passover they hanged Yeshu and the herald went out before him; for forty days he went out to announce, 'He is to be stoned on account of the fact that he practised sorcery and also enticed and tempted Israel astray; that knows a plea for defence for him, let him come and plead for his sake.' But they did not find a defence plea for him and they hanged him on the eve of Passover.

4. He went and raised Yeshu from the dead by necromancy.

He said to him 'Who is considered worthy in that world?'

He replied to him 'Israel'.

'What is necessary to join them?'

He replied to him 'Care for their good, do not care for their harm; anyone who touches them, it is as if he touches the pupil of his eye.'

5. 'And such-and-such? What about him in the world to come?'

He replied to them, 'It seems that you have not asked about anything except such-and-such.' And it wasn't that Rabbi Eliezer was disregarding them, but he did not declare a saying unless he had heard it in his days.[1]

6. ... and he replied to him, 'Akiba, you made me remember; there was one time where I was walking in the uppermost market

* This passage continues with an account of each of them being sentenced to death.

with Jude); 'Netser' is very likely derived from the root 'Nazar' and not an apostle at all; 'Buni' might suggest 'Boanerges', the nickname of James and John. It is a very obscure list.

The third passage is distinctly at odds with gospel accounts: hanging may be a loose term for crucifixion, and John agrees this took place on the eve of the Passover. But the intention to stone Jesus, and the herald's forty days are most surprising elements, and equally the plea for a defence that could not be found. Jesus' alleged practice of sorcery would reflect his wonder-working and may have been a charge used against him.

The remaining passages relate to the period after Jesus' death. Not much significance attaches to the first of these except the total absence of hostility to Jesus. The theme of the last remark is derived from Leviticus 19.18 and found in all the synoptics.[2]

Rabbi Eliezer was born not long after Jesus' death and was associated in the minds of other rabbis with some kind of flirtation with Christianity, of which he clearly had knowledge. Elsewhere, he talks of a man who would 'rise up and seek to make himself God, and to cause the whole world to go astray', but he attracted suspicion.

Here, in the fifth passage he is quietly defensive about Jesus' prospects in the world to come, while in the sixth, he encounters a man in Sepphoris, who might conceivably be James the Just, and quotes Jesus' teaching[3] to him.

of Sepphoris and I encountered one of the pupils of Yeshu the Nazarene, and Jacob, a man of Kefar Sekaniah, was his name. He said to me, "It is written in your Torah: 'You will not bring a harlot's pay . . .'; what about making a toilet for the high priest from it?"'

And I did not say anything to him. 'Thus Yeshu the Nazarene taught me: "She gathered it from a harlot's pay, and it returns to a harlot's pay: they came from a place of filth, to a place of filth they will go."'

And the saying pleased me; on account of this I was seized for heresy.

7. It happened to Rabbi Eliezer that a snake bit him and Jacob, a man of Kefar Sama, came to heal him in the name of Yeshu Ben Pantera; and Rabbi Ishmael did not let him; they said to him, 'You are not permitted, Ben Dama.' He said to him, 'I will produce proof for you that he may heal me.'

But he did not have time to produce the proof before he died. Rabbi Ishmael said, 'Happiness is yours, Ben Dama, because you depart in peace and you did not break down the decrees of the wise; as for all those that break the fences of the wise, in the end punishment comes upon them . . .'[4]

In the last passage we see a Christian coming to heal a rabbi in the name of Yeshu Ben Pantera but being prevented.

When we remember that the Christians came into being as Jewish heretics, the Talmud offers little in the way of condemnation of the new sect while reiterating the belief that Jesus was the son of an adulteress. These early statements are an important record of the way Jesus and his followers were perceived.

XX

CELSUS

Mary's occupation; her becoming pregnant by Panthera; Jesus' secret birth; he is hired for work in Egypt and learns magic there

Hand in hand with the Christian apologists of the second century went the anti-Christian polemicists, whom in some cases the apologists were attempting directly to answer. The satirist Lucian was one of these with his gibes at the 'crucified sophist' and Christian naivety and ignorance; another was the imperial tutor, Fronto of Cirta, dismissing the Christian love-feasts as orgies; and Numenius was a third, though we do not have any details of his attacks.

But by far the most sustained polemic was written by a Roman Platonist called Celsus and published in the late AD 170s. His writings would be altogether lost if they had not been quoted by Origen, who penned eight books 'Against Celsus' some 70 years afterwards.

The stormy and difficult life of this great scholar was punctuated by the publication of numerous works especially on textual criticism of the Bible, and theological exposition.

After this he [Celsus] presents a Jew in dialogue with Jesus himself who accuses him of many things . . . and first that he fabricated his birth from a virgin . . . he came from a village of Judaea, born to a poor country woman who earned her living by spinning . . . Jesus' mother was turned out by the carpenter betrothed to her, after being convicted of adultery and becoming pregnant by a soldier named Panthera . . .[1] a shameless vagabond, she gave birth to Jesus in secret . . . obliged by poverty to go to work in Egypt, he [Jesus] there acquired certain powers, in which the Egyptians pride themselves, and returned over-confident – by reason of these powers proclaiming himself God . . .

Gathering ten or eleven infamous men about him, tax-collectors and sailors of the most wretched kind, he fled with them this way and that, collecting the means to live in disgraceful, importunate ways . . . How could we consider him as God who . . . did not bring about anything that he promised, and when we had convicted and condemned him and judged him worthy of punishment, he hid himself and attempted shameful flight but was caught after betrayal by those he called his disciples?. . . A good general in command of thousands of soldiers is never betrayed, nor even a wicked leader of brigands . . . But Jesus, betrayed by his subordinates, did not command like a good general, and, having deceived his disciples, he did not inspire in them the goodwill . . . that robbers feel towards their leader . . .

I have many things to say on events in Jesus' life – accurate but differing from what Jesus' disciples have written – but I willingly put them to one side . . .[2] The Jew accuses the disciples of having made up the statement that Jesus knew in advance and predicted all that happened to

Very little has survived. He died not long after severe torture in the Decian persecution of AD 250–51.

Celsus displays considerable knowledge of the New Testament texts and, in his commentary on Jesus' life, repeats familiar themes – about his mother's affair and ejection (by Joseph?), Jesus' secret and ignominious birth, and his magical practices learned in Egypt, where poverty had forced him to go for work.

It has been the traditional Christian point of view to reject all this as nonsense. But Celsus' mention of Panthera – also named as Jesus' father in the Talmud – might point us towards the knowledge that there really was a soldier, with that unusual name about that time, whose first-century tombstone at Bingerbrück in Germany records him as an archer of Sidon, sixty-two years old.

The polarization of Christian and anti-Christian sentiment should not blind us to the fact that absolute truth does not necessarily lie in either camp.

him . . . Since he predicted who would betray him and who would deny him, how did they not fear him as God and cease from the betrayal and denial? If these things had been decreed for him . . . why does he lament and mourn and pray to avoid the fear of death, expressing himself with words like these: 'O Father, if this cup could pass from me!' . . . When he was on earth, he won over only ten or eleven most contemptible sailors and tax-collectors, and not even all of these . . . He did not help himself while alive, but when dead he rose again and showed the marks of his punishment and how his hands had been pierced. Who saw it? An hysterical woman . . .[3] and perhaps some other of those similarly bewitched.

XXI

JOSEPHUS

The death of Festus puts Jesus' brother's life in danger; account of Jesus; an Egyptian prophet; the Mount of Olives

Born in AD 37, an aristocratic Jew, Pharisee and priest, the important historian Josephus was appointed joint governor of Galilee in AD 66. The following year, defending Jotapata against the Romans besieging it, he was at length captured after engaging in activities described by G. A. Williamson as 'surely the most appalling story of cowardice, duplicity, and treason ever penned' – and penned by himself! Henceforth, he was to live among the Romans, though remaining a devoted defender of Jewish culture and religion.

His most famous work, *The Jewish War*, appeared at the end of the AD 70s, and *The Jewish Antiquities* in AD 93–4, from which the following extracts are taken.

The first of these sets the scene for the death of James, the brother of Jesus, as recorded by Hegesippus – telling how the Sadducee High Priest Ananus took advantage of the interval between the death of the Judaean governor Festus[1] and the arrival of his successor.

1. On learning of the death of Festus, the Emperor sent Albinus as governor to Judaea.* The younger Ananus, who as I have already mentioned had become High Priest, was an unusually forthright and bold character. He followed the sect of the Sadducees, who are the most harsh of all the Jews in their judgments, as I have already shown. Ananus, being the sort of man that he was, thought that he had an ideal opportunity, with Festus dead and Albinus still en route. He summoned a council of judges; brought before it the brother of Jesus, the so-called Christ, whose name was James, and some others, accused them of breaking the law and condemned them to be stoned. All those reputed to be the most reasonable people in the city, and those who were strict in matters of law, were very angry at this, and they secretly sent a message to the king asking him to instruct Ananus not to behave like this any more; indeed, they said, he had acted improperly right from the start. Some of them also went to Albinus on his way from Alexandria, and told him that it was illegal for Ananus to summon a council without his permission. Albinus was persuaded by what they said and wrote an angry letter to Ananus, threatening to punish him. It was because of this that King Herod Agrippa deprived Ananus of the High Priesthood after he had held it for three months, appointing Jesus son of Dammaeus instead.

2. And at this time arose Jesus – a wise man, if indeed one should call him a man. For he was a doer of extraordinary deeds and teacher of those who receive the truth with pleasure. And he won over many Jews and

* I follow Eusebius in omitting a passage here on the promotion of the younger Ananus by Herod Agrippa (Agrippa II), and some details of Ananus' father's family.

Elsewhere, Josephus is quoted as saying: 'These things happened to the Jews in vengeance for James the Just, who was the brother of Jesus, the so-called Christ, for they had put to death a man of outstanding integrity.' [2]

The expression 'so-called Christ' is clearly at odds with the second extract, from the *Antiquities*. Josephus might have altered his views in the intervening years, but the great scholar Origen did not know this passage, at least in its present form. The situation is not easily resoluble. Some have suggested that a more basic text has been adapted to be more in line with Christian thinking.[3] Others will say the whole text is an interpolation. We face a conundrum. But no one seems keen to allow the possibility that Josephus, by the time he published the *Antiquities*, could have written so sympathetic an account – despite the authority of our best manuscripts. In a recent development, a serious attempt has been made to link this passage with Luke 24.19–24, where Cleophas and his companion outline to a fellow-traveller (the resurrected Jesus) a record of Jesus' presence. Certain keywords suggest that Josephus' version may owe a considerable debt to this.

For the last passage we must turn to events in the AD 50s. Accused by the Jews of offences against the law, Paul was being brought before Felix, procurator of Judaea, when the Roman officer, in whose custody he was held, thought he recognized him and asked (Acts 21.38), 'Are you not that many Greeks as well. This was the Christ. And, on the indictment of the chief men amongst us, Pilate sentenced him to crucifixion, but those who had loved him from the beginning did not fall away. For he appeared to them alive again on the third day, the divine prophets having foretold these and countless other wonderful things in respect of him. And even now the tribe of Christians (taking their name from him) is not at an end.

3. At this time someone arrived in Jerusalem from Egypt, claiming to be a prophet and counselling the mass of common people to go with him to the mountain called the Mount of Olives, which lies opposite the city at a distance of five furlongs. For he said he wanted to demonstrate to them from this place that at his command the walls of Jerusalem would fall, and he promised to provide them with an entrance through these. When Felix learned of this he ordered his soldiers to take up their arms. And hastening from Jerusalem with many troops of cavalry and infantry, he fell upon the Egyptian's entourage and killed four hundred of them, taking two hundred alive. But the Egyptian[4] himself fled from the battle and disappeared . . .

Egyptian who formerly caused an uproar and led out into the desert 4,000 men who were murderers?'

It is a very odd fact that, within some twenty years of Jesus' death in the early AD 30s, someone else should have been active in Judaea who, in several respects, strongly resembled him. We are very fortunate in having two separate accounts by Josephus of this man, whose name we do not know. Like Jesus he was a prophet – or so he declared himself to be; he came out of Egypt, where Jewish sources and in particular Celsus also declared Jesus to have spent some time; he led his followers to the Mount of Olives, where Jesus also preached; and his last action was a mission with his followers into Jerusalem. This man may have been the same as a Ben Stada mentioned in the Talmud[5] as having brought magical practices from Egypt. But, whether or not this is so, the Egyptian seems to have contributed to a deliberate confusion or misunderstanding about Jesus that, in the minds of many, dogged Christians for centuries. The fourth-century Arnobius could write: 'My opponent will perhaps meet me with many other slanderous and childish accusations that are commonly urged: Jesus was a Magus; he accomplished all these things by secret arts. From the Egyptians' shrines he stole the names of angels of power, and the religious system of a distant country. Fools, why speak of things you have not examined and that remain unknown to you . . .?'[6]

XXII

SUETONIUS

Christians battle with the Jews at Rome? Their banishment

In Acts 18.2 we read that Paul met a Jew named Aquila, 'lately come from Italy, with his wife Priscilla: because Claudius had commanded all Jews to depart from Rome . . .'

This event, from from AD 49 must surely be the same as that recorded by the Roman historian, Suetonius, in his *Lives of the Caesars* published *c.* AD 121; we do not know the reasons for Claudius' decision, but it was very likely a consequence of the never-ceasing hostility of the Jews of the orthodox faith to the proponents of the new religion. It is certainly odd, however, if so good a historian as Suetonius misspelt Christ's name or thought that he was still alive.

Since the Jews were continu-
ally causing trouble under the
influence of Chrestus, he
[Claudius] expelled them from
Rome.

XXIII

TACITUS

Nero's horrifying treatment of the Christians

This greatest of Roman historians and gifted writer of complex, sophisticated Latin was born *c.* AD 55 and lived into the second century, when his *Annals*, from which the following extract is taken, were published. In his account of the great fire of Rome in the summer of AD 64, he clearly does not believe the Christians were the real culprits and probably shared the developing resentment against Nero's[1] savagery. But there is no doubting that he believed Christianity was foul,[2] its adherents appalling and deserving of the harshest penalties under the law.

It is not easy for us to understand the immense hostility shown to Christianity by the Romans. But it would seem that many rumours were flying around about their 'secret' practices – such as infanticide,[3] orgies[4] and cannibalism[5] (this last derived from the ritual instituted at the Last Supper). In addition, the charge of atheism was levelled at them, since they refused all worship to Roman gods.

But neither human assistance nor the emperor's largesse nor propitiations of the gods served to allay the scandal of the belief that the fire had been ordered. So, to end the rumour, Nero set up as the guilty parties, inflicting upon them the most refined punishments, those hated for their abominations who were commonly called Christians. Christ, who gave them their name, had been executed by the procurator Pontius Pilate when Tiberius was emperor. Though temporarily controlled, the pernicious superstition broke out again not only in Judaea where that evil had originated but in that city [i.e. Rome] where all dreadful and shocking things gather from every part and find acceptance. So first those who confessed were arrested, then on their evidence a huge number were convicted less for the charge of arson than of hatred for the human race. And they died exposed to mockery – torn to death by hounds while covered in the hides of wild beasts, or crucified or, as fit for the flames, when daylight failed being burned as nightlights. Nero had offered his gardens for that display and staged a circus show, mingling with the people dressed as a charioteer or driving his chariot. For which reason a feeling of pity began to develop, even for those who were guilty, and worthy of extreme punishment – apparently being destroyed not for public benefit but for one man's cruelty.

XXIV

THE SLAVONIC
VERSION OF JOSEPHUS

**Account of Jesus; Pilate questions and
releases him; Pilate succumbs to a bribe;
was Jesus resurrected?**

Just over one hundred years ago Alexander Berendts began
his publication of an Old Slavonic version of Josephus'
The Jewish War preserved in a variety of Russian and other
manuscripts dating from the fifteenth century. This version
was hugely at variance with the traditional Greek text thanks
to a number of omissions and additions. And some of these
additions were unusually interesting for content relating to
the beginnings of Christianity.

There has been a huge debate over the authenticity of
the Christian entries, but one important theory proposed
that the differences are explained by Josephus' releasing of
a first edition – originally in Aramaic, then translated into
Greek – in the reign of the emperor Titus (AD 79–81).[1] This
might have been radically altered for his second edition,
published in the reign of Titus' unstable and bloodthirsty

1. A man appeared at that time if it is right to call him a man,[2] human in form and nature, super-human in his appearance and activities. Such were the great and extraordinary miracles he per-formed that I cannot call him a man . . . His commanding words enabled him to do all he did, out of some unseen power. There were those who said the first law-giver [i.e. Moses] had come alive again to employ many healing arts; others declared that he came from God. But he was often dis-senting from the law, not observing traditional Sabbath practice, while avoiding uncleanness and using his words only, not his hands. He had many followers who came to re-ceive instruction from him. Many were inspired by the belief that the Jews would break free from the Romans. He used to be found on the Mount of Olives, where he would heal people. 150 acolytes and many others became his ad-herents, seeing the power of his words to fulfil his wishes.

They requested him to go into Jerusalem, kill Pilate and the Romans and make himself their king. But he rejected this idea. After the Jewish leaders heard about this, they went before the high priest, declaring they were too weak to oppose the Romans: 'Let us remove our worries (they said) by telling Pilate what we have learned, for if he hears it from anyone else, we will lose our property and our lives, and our children will be sent into exile.' So they went and told Pilate, who had his troops kill many of the people and Jesus brought in. Pilate's enquiries led him to understand that Jesus was a benefactor, not a wrongdoer, and certainly not a rebel in search of kingship. So he let him go – he had cured Pilate's wife at the point of death.

He returned to his old haunts and his customary activities. More people gathered about him. And once more he won exceptional renown. The lawyers were deeply resentful and bribed Pilate with brother Domitian (AD 81–96) who was concerned about the Christians and launched a persecution *c.* AD 95.

It has been rightly said[3] that the author of the following passages is revealed 'not as a believer but as a doubting, if curious, onlooker' – a description that might well fit Josephus, who was neither Christian nor anywhere evidently hostile to Christianity.

With a wealth of information, some of it supported by other known texts (e.g. 4 – a prediction also recorded by Suetonius and Tacitus and by Josephus himself in the familiar text of *The Jewish War*), and some of it in contradiction (e.g. Pilate's massacre at the time of Jesus' first apprehension, and his acceptance of a huge bribe), it is not easy to believe this could be the work of any medieval author, Christian or otherwise.

Perhaps we are really in the presence of the first non-Christian witness to write about Jesus at any length and with any understanding. But more research is needed, and we are short of any confident conclusions. In the meantime these fascinating texts will continue to be the subject of fierce debate.[4]

30 talents to kill him. He yielded to the bribe but left them to carry out their wishes themselves.[5] And they crucified Jesus, in offence against their own law, greatly reviling him.

2. And above these [inscriptions in Greek, Roman and Jewish on the law of purity and banning of gentiles] a fourth hung, in the letters of those languages, proclaiming that Jesus, the king who had not reigned, was crucified by the Jews for prophesying the destruction of the City and total demolition of the Temple.

3. Before the current generation this curtain had been intact by virtue of the people's piety. But now it was a wretched sight, having been suddenly split in two, when the doer of good, a man whose actions made him more than man, was delivered to be executed in return for a bribe. They tell of many other extraordinary events at that time: after his execution and burial his body went missing from the tomb. Some claimed he had risen; others that his friends had stolen him.[6] I am not sure which version is nearer the truth. A dead man cannot rise except assisted by the prayer of another righteous man – unless he be an angel or heavenly power or God Himself, appearing like a man amongst men, fulfilling his intentions, and dying and being buried and rising as he chooses. Others declared it was impossible to remove him, for there were guards posted around his tomb, 30* Romans and 1,000 Jews.

4. But they were induced to go to war by a doubtful prediction in the sacred books, declaring that in those times someone from Judaea would reign over the whole world. There are various explanations, some believing it referred to Herod, others to the crucified miracle-worker, Jesus, and others to Vespasian.

* Or, 1,000

XXV

IMPERIAL POLICY

Whether or when Christians should be punished; how one should respond to informers

The beginnings of imperial policy on Christianity are possibly traceable even to the time of Tiberius who died in AD 37, only two or three years after Jesus. Shortly before AD 200, Tertullian, a Christian author from Africa, records in his *Apology* that Tiberius[1] reported to the Senate his own endorsement of Jesus, which was rejected by them; whereupon Tiberius delivered a threat against Christian accusers. This story is hardly credible, though if Tiberius had had communication with Pontius Pilate or his wife, who returned from Pilate's administration in AD 36 after complaints, it is also not impossible.[2] The numbers of Christians would have been very tiny, and even their title had not yet been formalized.[3]

The hostility of Nero and of Domitian are recorded elsewhere in this volume (see Tacitus and Hegesippus). But it would seem that the Christians, relatively untroubled by

1. *Caius Plinius Secundus, governor of Bithynia, writes to the emperor Trajan in AD 112 concerning official Roman policy on how to deal with Christians.*

Master, it is my usual practice to consult you on all matters about which I am not certain. For who is better able (than you) to resolve my difficulties and cure my lack of knowledge?

I have never been present at courts of inquiry concerning Christians; consequently I am unaware what form the inquiry should take and what range of punishments is usual. I have agonized quite a lot over whether there should be any allowance made for age or whether the young should be treated differently from more mature people: whether forgiveness should be afforded to those who recant, or whether it is of no benefit for someone, who has been a Christian through and through, to have ceased to be; or whether the title 'Christian' should be punished per se, if there is no wrongdoing involved, or only the wrongdoing which is associated with the title.

For the moment, in regard to those who have been brought before me as Christians, I have taken the following approach: I have asked them whether they are Christians. If they say they are, I have asked them a second and third time, making it clear they face the death penalty. If they continue in the claim, I have ordered them to be taken away for execution. I have no doubt that, whatever it was they were confessing to, such stubborn pig-headedness should be punished. Some who maintained this foolish stance, I have put on the list for deportation to Rome, because they were full citizens.

Before long, as often happens, because I had got involved with this, more instances of this widespread malaise have emerged. An anonymous document containing the names of several suspects

Roman persecution in the AD 40s and 50s, were – perhaps from AD 64, when they were treated as arsonists – routinely arrested and tried on the grounds that all Christians were troublemakers, though the individual policy of governors would vary. The relatively humane and decent emperors of the early second century, connected with the following documents, are trying to operate the law fairly. But there is no doubting that they see the Christians as a potential source of mischief.

has been brought to my attention. With regard to those who said they were not Christians and never had been, I began a prayer to the gods and they joined in; when I had your statue brought in and placed alongside those of the gods, they worshipped it, as I had intended, with offerings of incense and wine; furthermore they insulted Christ, which those who are really Christians cannot be made to do; those then, I considered should be allowed to go free. Others, indicted by the informer, said they were Christians and before long said they weren't; some, that they had been but had ceased to be some three years before, some a lot longer than that and one or two even twenty years ago. All of those too worshipped your statue and the images of the gods and insulted Christ. They claimed that the sum total of their misguided involvement had been to congregate before it was light on a particular day and chant responses in honour of Christ, as if he was a god, and bind themselves by an oath. It wasn't an oath to commit crimes. No, it was an oath, not to rob or steal, not to commit adultery, not to break their word and not to refuse to pay back a loan when it was due. After they had completed these rituals, they said that it was their custom to disperse and to re-assemble later to eat a meal together, but a meal that was ordinary and harmless.[4] They said that they had given up doing this as a result of my edict, by which, according to your official instructions, I had banned political gatherings.

All this made me think that it was advisable to interrogate under torture two female slaves, who were spoken of as 'deaconesses', to find out where the truth lay.[5] All I found was evidence of an ill-founded and extreme belief.

As a result of all this, I have put the inquiry on hold and lost no time in getting in touch with you. I thought it needed looking at, particularly because of the numbers of people at risk of involvement. People of all ages, of every class, of both sexes, in great numbers are being exposed to the risk and will continue to be in the future. It isn't only the urban areas which have been tainted by this contamination, but the villages and country districts as well. But I do think it can be checked and eradicated. It is common knowledge that temples, which in recent times have been empty, are now starting to fill up again; religious practices, long neglected, are being revived and, whereas recently hardly anyone was buying meat for sacrifices, it is now on sale everywhere. The obvious conclusion to be drawn from this is that lots of people can be freed from contamination, if they are given an opportunity to recant.

The Emperor Trajan replies:

My dear Secundus, you have followed the correct procedure in investigating the cases of Christians who have been brought before you. There is no general rule which can be applied to every case. They should not be subjected to a 'witch hunt'. If they are brought before you and proved guilty, they should be punished, with the proviso that, if someone has said he is not a Christian and backed it up by his actions, that is by praying to our gods, even if previously he had been under suspicion, he should gain pardon by recanting. Let me make it clear that anonymous documents have no place in our judicial system. They set a very bad precedent and are not something which my rule will tolerate.

2. *Letter from the Emperor Hadrian to Minucius Fundanus:* that we should not be persecuted without trial.*[6]

I have received a letter from your distinguished predecessor

Serennius Granianus.* I do not think that the matter should be left without being investigated, otherwise the men will be harassed and informers will be allowed to work mischief. Now if the provincials are so confident in their petition as to be able to answer in a court of law, let them rely on this alone, and not on petitions and mere out-cries. For it is much more suitable that you should be the judge whenever someone wants to bring an accusation. If an accu-sation is brought, and it is proved that these people have acted illegally, then you must pass judgement according to the grav-ity of the offence. But if anyone brings a case for personal advan-tage, then in heaven's name arrest him for his audacity and see to it that he gets punished.

* Their names should be Gaius Minicius Fundanus and Quintus Licinius Silvanus Granianus.

151

XXVI

OTHER TEXTS

There was lately published the translation of a Coptic text entitled The Gospel of Judas taken from a manuscript supposedly found *c.* 1978 in Middle Egypt. This remarkable work, exalting Judas Iscariot above the other apostles and claiming that he was requested by Jesus to betray him, has real interest for its independent stance. But it belongs within the Gnostic tradition – perhaps the work condemned by Irenaeus as emanating from the Cainites, who were alleged to be the champions of a number of Biblical characters usually disesteemed. Regrettably, such a text has no place in the current volume, since it has no apparent value either for its historical content or for any light it throws on the teachings or life of Jesus.

There is a simply vast body of apocryphal works of this kind, for a variety of reasons falsifying the truth or misleading. A few of these deserve mention since at some time or another they have gained a general currency:

- The letters of Paul and Seneca;
- The letters of Christ and Abgarus;
- Letters connected with Pilate (who must have filed an official report on the circumstances of Jesus' death, but this has not survived); and
- Paul's Epistle to the Laodiceans.

For the reader's interest, I have included *St Paul's Third Epistle to the Corinthians*, in the translation that Lord Byron made out of the Latin and Armenian, in the Convent of St Lazzaro in 1817.

There were several fabrications of Christian history and teaching even in the last century, which are passed over in silence. Nor should it be thought that apocryphal literature is at an end. The Nag Hammadi Library presented a whole new body of such writings in the mid-twentieth century and, as late as 1991, the Gospel of the Saviour was identified in Berlin by an American scholar.

Some of these writings one can appreciate for their fictional merits – who will forget the famous story of Quo Vadis, in which Jesus confronts Peter in flight from Rome?[1] The Infancy Gospel of Thomas has stories about Jesus' childhood that one might certainly wish to be true. They might even *be* true. But it would be impossible to justify their inclusion as historical material.

A late story of real merit is preserved in a single medieval manuscript – apparently a copy of a ninth-century *Life of Mary Magdalene* by the scholar Rabanus Maurus. It tells how Mary, temporarily settled at Aix in France and acknowledged as the special friend of the Saviour, would spread the Christian message not by speech alone: 'She would point to her eyes as those which had washed with her tears the feet of her Saviour, and had seen Him first when He rose from the dead – to her hair which had wiped His sacred feet – to her lips which had kissed them, not only during His life here, but even after His death and resurrection – to her hands which had touched them and anointed them . . .'[2] But do we believe this? How do we determine?

The traditions of Clement of Alexandria, however, being so much nearer in date to the events they profess to portray, seem more authentic. One of these concerns the death of James, the brother of John: his accuser was so moved by his testimony that he declared himself a Christian, and as they headed together for their place of execution, he sought James' forgiveness. James paused, before replying that he wished him peace, and kissed him.

In another story of Clement's, Peter saw his wife led away to execution ahead of him. Clement records Peter's joy and the encouraging and comforting way in which he spoke to her.

Two fragmentary works with Peter's name attached to them command our interest for their early date. *The Preaching of Peter* is quoted from by Clement and Origen. The latter comments that it is neither reckoned among the books of the church nor by Peter. But it is certainly intriguing for Jesus' declaring his injunction to the apostles against 'going out into the world' for twelve years.

The Gospel of Peter, possibly of Syrian origin, was altogether lost until its 1886/7 rediscovery in Egypt in a tomb at Akhmim. Serapion of Antioch (*c.* AD 200) had read it, so that we may confidently ascribe it to the second century, and probably the middle of that century. Its particular interest is in providing the earliest full account of the passion and resurrection outside the New Testament. Since it draws upon Matthew, Luke and John at separate points in the narration without real differences, it cannot really be considered an independent source. Mary Magdalene is named as the leader of the women who visited the tomb on the morning of the resurrection. The drawing of the nails from Jesus' hands is another surprising detail.

At about the same date that the Gospel of Peter was written, Justin Martyr (*c.* AD 100–165), a philosopher who converted to Christianity, was penning his *Apologies* to the Emperor Marcus Aurelius as well as his defence of Christianity against Judaism, the *Dialogue with Trypho*. In the course of these works two statements are noteworthy; first, he assigns to Jesus the same employment as Joseph: he is a carpenter, a maker of ploughs and yokes. (But this might be an elaboration of Mark 6.3.) Second, he offers a variant of the nativity story: how Joseph, unable to find a room in the village, put up in a cave nearby. There Mary gave birth to Jesus and laid him in a manger, where the Magi[3] (from Arabia) found him.

The cave nearby might very well be the inn of Chimham by Bethlehem, which had a long history as a point of departure for travellers to Egypt.[4] Jerome, who lived at Bethlehem, knew stories both of this cave[5] and of other sites connected with Jesus' birth. Perhaps we are entitled to speculate: did Joseph really travel to Bethlehem with his heavily pregnant wife and why? And were they about to cross into Egypt? (The two gospel narratives of the nativity, Luke's and Matthew's, are strongly in conflict.)

In a beautiful story recorded by Plutarch, a ship's pilot in the time of Tiberius seems to have heard the mourning chant of Tammuz's followers as the vessel passed the Greek island of Paxi. This was later interpreted as the death of paganism in the face of Christianity.

Two women remote from the Christian hierarchy should also be mentioned here for perhaps connected reasons. We read in Tacitus' *Annals* that Pomponia Graecina was the wife of Aulus Plautius, the general who conquered Southern Britain in Claudius' invasion of AD 43. She was accused of 'atheism' in AD 57 and handed over to her husband for trial, who pronounced her innocent. The suggestion that 'atheism' here means Christianity seems supported by third-century Christian inscriptions relating to the *gens Pomponia*.

Now in Paul's second epistle to Timothy, two Christians, Pudens and Claudia, are mentioned. Are these identical with the Pudens and Claudia mentioned as husband and wife in the epigrams of the Roman poet Martial? If so, Claudia can be identified as a Briton. And she may have come to Rome in the conqueror's retinue, and met his wife. Though unprovable, this is not far-fetched. (From a Romano-British inscription we are encouraged to believe Claudia the daughter of a British king Cogidumnus.)

Two other authorities – Thallus and Phlegon – each refer to an eclipse considered, the one by Julius Africanus and the other by Origen, to be identical with the darkness associated with the crucifixion. Thallus wrote a history in three books and may possibly be the same as a Samaritan of that name who lent Agrippa, king of Judaea in AD 41, a large sum of money shortly before his becoming ruler. At any rate, Thallus calls 'this darkness' an eclipse of the sun, while Phlegon, a freedman of the emperor Hadrian, records that it happened in the time of Tiberius (AD 14–37)[6] and mentions also earthquakes occurring at that time, named as the time of Jesus' Passion (Origen II.59).

Origen knew that Phlegon had also referred to certain successful predictions made by Jesus but that he had unfortunately muddled Jesus with Peter.

Another early writer, Mara bar Serapion, wrote a surviving Syriac letter sometime after his flight from Samosata when it was conquered by Vespasian in AD 73. In the course of this letter he writes: 'Or what profit had the Jews from the execution of their wise king, seeing that from that time forward the kingdom was taken away from them?'[7]

Among later accounts, it is interesting to note Peter's diet as recorded by the fourth-century Gregory Nazianzen, who remarks on his great temperance and abstinence: he would eat daily, for a negligible sum of money, an unpleasant and bitter kind of pulse, varying his diet occasionally with herbs; on certain occasions he would eat what was put in front of him.

Finally, there is Jerome's story of John, now ancient and decrepit. On his way to the church gatherings, he would repeat only, 'Little children, love one another,' which began to vex his listeners, who asked him why he said nothing else. His answer was that it was the Lord's command and that if they did nothing else this alone was enough.

APPENDIX I

A SPECIMEN OF AN APOCRYPHAL TEXT

(Referred to in 'Other Texts'): The 3rd Epistle of Paul to the Corinthians*

1. Paul, in bonds for Jesus Christ, disturbed by so many errors, to his Corinthian brethren, health.

2. I nothing marvel that the preachers of evil have made this progress.

3. For because the Lord Jesus is about to fulfil his coming, verily on this account do certain men pervert and despise his words.

4. But I, verily, from the beginning, have taught you that only which I myself received from the former apostles, who always remained with the Lord Jesus Christ.

5. And I now say unto you, that the Lord Jesus Christ was born of the Virgin Mary, who was the seed of David.

6. According to the annunciation of the Holy Ghost, sent to her from our Father from heaven.

---

* This second-century attack on the Gnostic errors was long canonical with the Syrian church, and much longer still with the Armenian.

7. That Jesus might be introduced into the world and deliver our flesh by his flesh, and that he might raise us up from the dead.

8. As in this also he himself became the example.

9. That it might be made manifest that man was created by the Father.

10. He has not remained in perdition unsought.

11. But he is sought for, that he might be revived by adoption.

12. For God, who is the Lord of all, the Father of our Lord Jesus Christ, who made heaven and earth, sent, firstly, the Prophets to the Jews.

13. That he would absolve them from their sins, and bring them to his judgement.

14. Because he wished to save, firstly the house of Israel, he bestowed and poured forth his Spirit upon the Prophets.

15. That they should, for a long time, preach the worship of God, and the nativity of Christ.

16. But he who was the prince of evil, when he wished to make himself God, laid his hand upon them.

17. And bound all men in sin.

18. Because the judgement of the world was approaching.

19. But Almighty God, when he willed to justify, was unwilling to abandon his creature.

20. But, when he saw his affliction, he had compassion upon him.

21. And at the end of a time he sent the Holy Ghost into the Virgin foretold by the Prophets.

22. Who, believing readily was made worthy to conceive, and bring forth our Lord Jesus Christ.

23. That from this perishable body, in which the evil spirit was glorified, he should be cast out, and it should be made manifest.

24. That he was not God: For Jesus Christ in his flesh, had recalled and saved this perishable flesh, and drawn it into eternal life by faith.

25. Because in his body he would prepare a pure temple of justice for all ages.

26. In whom we also, when we believe, are saved.

27. Therefore know ye, that these men are not the children of justice, but the children of wrath.

28. Who turn away from themselves the compassion of God.

29. Who say that neither the heavens nor the earth were altogether works made by the hand of the Father of all things.

30. But these cursed men have the doctrine of the serpent.

31. But do ye, by the power of God, withdraw yourselves far from these, and expel from amongst you the doctrine of the wicked.

32. Because you are not the children of rebellion but the sons of the beloved church.

33. And on this account the time of the resurrection is preached to all men.

34. Therefore they who affirm that there is no resurrection of the flesh, they indeed shall not be raised up to eternal life.

35. But to Judgement and condemnation shall the unbeliever arise in the flesh.

36. For to that body which denies the resurrection of the body, shall be denied the resurrection: because such are found to refuse the resurrection.

37. But you also, Corinthians! have known, from the seeds of wheat, and from other seeds.

38. That one grain falls dry into the earth, and within it first dies.

39. And afterwards rises again, by the will of the Lord, endued with the same body.

40. Neither indeed does it rise with the same simple body, but manifold, and filled with blessing.

41. But we produce the example not only from seeds but from the honourable bodies of men.

42. Ye have also known Jonas, the son of Amittai.

43. Because he delayed to preach to the Ninevites, he was swallowed up in the belly of a fish for three days and three nights.

44. And after three days God heard his supplication, and brought him out of the deep abyss.

45. Neither was any part of his body corrupted; neither was his eyebrow bent down.

46. And how much more for you, oh men of little faith.

47. If you believe in our Lord Jesus Christ, will he raise you up, even as he himself hath arisen.

48. If the bones of Elisha the prophet, falling upon the dead, revived the dead.

49. By how much more shall ye, who are supported by the flesh and blood and the Spirit of Christ, arise again on that day with a perfect body?

50. Elias the prophet, embracing the widow's son, raised him from the dead.

51. By how much more shall Jesus Christ revive you, on that day, with a perfect body, even as he himself hath arisen?

52. But if ye receive other things vainly.

53. Henceforth no one shall cause me to travail; for I bear on my body these fetters.

54. To obtain Christ; and I suffer with patience these afflictions to become worthy of the resurrection of the dead.

55. And do each of you, having received the law from the hands of the blessed Prophets and the holy gospel, firmly maintain it.

56. To the end that you may be rewarded in the resurrection of the dead, and the possession of the life eternal.

57. But if any of ye, not believing, shall trespass, he shall be judged with the misdoers, and punished with those who have false belief.

58. Because such are the generation of vipers, and the children of dragons and basilisks.

59. Drive far from amongst ye, and fly from such, with the aid of our Lord Jesus Christ.

60. And the peace and grace of the beloved Son be upon you. Amen.

APPENDIX II

CHRISTIANITY AND THE FAMILY OF JESUS

Jesus is recorded in the gospels as having four brothers and at least two sisters, but there is some real confusion with members of the family of Cleophas and his wife, another Mary. If, as Hegesippus records, Cleophas was the brother of Joseph, perhaps the two families lived together – most likely after Joseph's death.

I suggest the 'brothers' and 'sisters' were really first cousins of Jesus,[1] (though Paul [Gal.1.19], Josephus, Jude and Hegesippus offer evidence to support a belief that James and Jude, at least, were half or full brothers) and by equations linking the names Cleophas, Clopas and Alphaeus (a possible Greek form of the Aramaic name), we may find two of these, James and Judas (Jude) in the gospel list of apostles. Whether Simon the Zealot – follower of a fierce national independence party, perhaps the one founded in the year of the census at the time of Roman annexation – was also a cousin is more doubtful but possible.[2]

By another equation, it appears likely that the mother of Zebedee's children was called Salome.[3] Now John 19.25 mentions a sister of Jesus' mother. Might this be Salome, who evidently belonged to an inner circle of female followers?

If so, it was Jesus' aunt who was pleading for his first cousins to have prime places in heaven,[4] and a longtime closeness between Jesus and two of the three chief apostles, James and John, becomes probable.

There should therefore, for many years after Jesus' death, have been reliable traditions about Jesus extending far backwards beyond details of the ministry at the end of his life. In addition to James son of Zebedee executed in AD 42 and Jesus' mother, who probably did not outlive her son very far, his first cousins John and James (and Jude?)[5] remained as important family witnesses within the Christian community for many years. By this reckoning the first age of Christianity might be said to begin with Jesus' acceptance by his supposed second cousin, John the Baptist, and end with the death of his first cousin, John[6] son of Zebedee, last of the apostles.

Christian involvement of the Desposunoi – the Lord's people – continued with Jude's grandsons after their witness for Jesus in Domitian's reign. And Hegesippus even has a story of Symeon, son of Clopas, being martyred as both a member of David's family and a Christian in Trajan's reign after considerable torture.[7] The detail that he was 120 years old is not credible, but his survival into Trajan's reign, which began in AD 98, is reasonable – perhaps it was he who, as Clopas' companion, had met the resurrected Jesus on the road to Emmaus.[8] His death is placed *c.* 106.

These family members, carrying status as of the old royal house as well as by virtue of kinship with Jesus, were still thriving in the third century with three successive bishops of Seleucia on the Tigris; and another was Conon gardener of Magydus martyred in the Decian persecution (AD 250).

Conon seems to have been informed upon by the Jews; on being questioned by the governor Epolius, he is recorded as replying, 'I came from the town of Nazareth in Galilee, and am a kinsman of Christ.'[9]

Less than a century was to pass before Christianity became the de facto religion of the empire.

Suggested Genealogy of Jesus' family

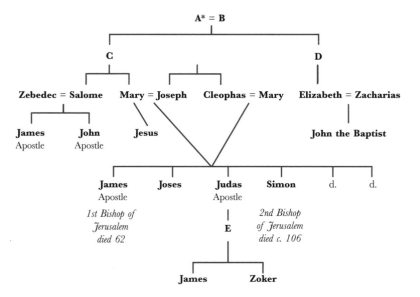

It has been postulated that James and perhaps others were children by a former marriage of Joseph's. But James would then claim precedence as heir to David so this is not likely.

* Letters A to E represent members of Jesus' family whose names remain unknown.

APPENDIX III

DESCRIPTION OF JESUS

The lengthy description of Jesus ascribed to one Lentulus – 'a man in stature middling tall, and comely, etc.' – is certainly apocryphal, and perhaps no earlier than medieval. This raises the interesting question: is there any reliable portraiture of Jesus?

Celsus claimed Jesus as 'small, ugly and ignoble'; while Origen would not assent to the first and third attributes, he agreed that the scriptures gave authority to the idea of Jesus' ugliness and quoted a prophecy of Isaiah in support. Many other earlier writers seem to have favoured this view (e.g. Irenaeus, Clement of Alexandria, Tertullian), and it is only rarely that he is described as handsome. Oddly, we have very late records of Luke having been a skilled painter and if this is true, it seems very likely that he would have portrayed Jesus and others among the first Christians. A fifth- or sixth-century record tells how a picture[1] of Jesus' mother by Luke was sent from Jerusalem to the empress Pulcheria at Byzantium, where it was placed in a church built by her in Mary's honour.

Eusebius had seen coloured portraits of Jesus, Paul and Peter. He also refers to the story in Mark 5.25–34 of the woman cured by Jesus of a haemorrhage. She was said to have come from the city of Caesarea Philippi, and where she had once lived there was still a 'wonderful memorial' left by the grateful patient: this took the form of a bronze statue of a woman on one knee in supplication before a man standing with hand stretched out to her, and a double cloak arranged neatly over his shoulder; Eusebius had seen this, and repeats the belief that the man's features resembled those of Jesus – but sadly offers no description.[2]

APPENDIX IV

CHRONOLOGY

(Some of these dates – especially relating to Jesus' life – are approximate.)

27 BC   Augustus becomes emperor.

7 BC[1]   Birth of Jesus. Though he appears to have been of a Nazareth family, Luke and Matthew concur on his birth at Bethlehem – whether in fulfilment of an Old Testament prophecy or for another reason.[1]

4 BC   Death of Herod the Great; Archelaus becomes ruler of Judaea and other territories.

AD 5[1]   Jesus debates with the priesthood in the Temple. The next 25 years of his life are lost except for the statement of Luke (2.51–52) and of the Jews/Celsus. (The tenth-century Arab historian Masudi knew of a Christian tradition that Jesus studied for many years in a synagogue in Tiberius.)*

AD 6   Census of Judaea carried out under the orders of Quirinius, governor of Syria, following the deposition of Archelaus and Roman annexation of his territory. (Presumably the census referred to in Luke 2.1–3).

* Jesus concluded his studying after he had a vision while reading the book of Isaiah.

In the parable of the pounds (Luke 19.12–27) Jesus surely refers to a client-king of Rome and may well be remembering the efforts of Archelaus to retain his throne when summoned to Rome to face charges in this year. He had certainly experienced, as in verse 14, the hatred of the citizens.

AD 14 Death of Augustus: Tiberius becomes emperor.

AD 27 Pontius Pilate becomes Procurator of Judaea.

AD 31 Baptism of Jesus by John the Baptist, whose acceptance of Jesus as the Christ and rite of baptism are his two certain contributions to Christianity.

AD 32 Execution of John the Baptist by (Herod) Antipas.[2] Shortly after, the very young Salome, daughter of Herodias, who is responsible for his death – Herodias had been offended with John for his condemning Antipas when he took her as his wife although already married – marries the tetrarch Philip and, after his death, Herod's great-grandson King Aristobulus of Chalcidene, who was still alive in the late AD 80s and possibly the AD 90s.

AD 34 Death of Philip, the tetrarch of the north-eastern districts (Luke 3.1) His principality was poor, but he cared deeply for his subjects, travelling around with a portable throne and carrying out instant process of justice on the road-side in answer to his subjects' complaints. John 6.15 might be seen as an attempt to fill the vacant tetrarchy if Jesus had crossed the Sea of Galilee into part of Philip's territory, Gaulanitis. Another odd passage (John 2.20) – naming the Temple (built between 20 and

12 BC) as completed after 46 years when the real figure was about 8 years – might be adapted to read 'This Temple has stood for 46 years . . .' This relates to the beginning of Jesus' ministry, and might point to AD 33 or 34, though such a date seems far too late.

AD 35   Execution of Jesus; Antipas sidesteps involvement, no doubt with the execution of John the Baptist still troubling him. A political consequence is the renewing of a damaged friendship between Antipas and Pilate.

AD 36   Pontius Pilate recalled after Samaritan complaints. Aretas IV, king of the Nabateans, attacks Antipas' territory and defeats his army. He is the father of the wife Antipas rejected for Herodias.

AD 37   Death of Tiberius.

AD 42   Execution of James, John's brother. (See Acts 12.1–2.)

AD 49   Expulsion of the Jews from Rome.

AD 52   Paul mistaken for the Egyptian.

AD 54–68   Nero emperor.

AD 62   Death of James the Just.

AD 64   Great fire at Rome; Christians accused of arson; execution of Peter.

AD 66   The Christians flee Jerusalem for Pella, in response, it is said, to an oracle.

AD 66–70   First Jewish war.

AD 67   Execution of Paul.

AD 65–85   Synoptic Gospels written, but Matthew's original text may be earlier.

AD 70   Jerusalem razed by Titus.

AD 73   Vespasian's persecution of the Jews.

AD 81–96   Domitian emperor.

AD 85–95   Gospel of John.

AD 95   Domitian's persecution of the Christians.

AD 96   First Epistle of Clement.

AD 98–117   Trajan emperor.

AD 100   Death of John, last of the apostles.

AD 107   Death of Ignatius; the original version of Polycarp's letter to the Philippians.

AD 117–38   Hadrian emperor; Quadratus' and Aristides' *Apologies*.

AD 135   Crushing of Barcochba's rebellion; Jerusalem rebuilt as Aelia Capitolina by Hadrian.

APPENDIX V

THE FAMILY OF HEROD

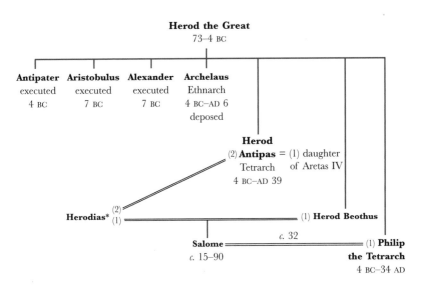

* Not married to Philip the Tetrarch as stated at *Matt 14.3*.

APPENDIX VI

GLOSSARY

Apocrypha (of the New Testament) A multitude of early Christian documents not admitted into the canon. These are generally distinguished by bogus authorship or content, i.e. for a variety of reasons they make unjustified and untrue claims for themselves.

Apostle Jesus is supposed to have selected an inner circle of twelve followers, though confusion over names can leave even this number doubtful. Possibly these were originally intended as emissaries for the twelve tribes of Israel. (James' epistle is written to the tribes.) Interestingly, there was a decision to replace Judas Iscariot (with Matthias); and lastly Paul accorded himself this title. The Jews and Celsus are curiously vague about this inner circle, perhaps deliberately.

Canon The admitted books of the New Testament.

Chrestus The name used by Suetonius for the leader of the disturbances that led to the Jews' expulsion from Rome. It is believed to refer to Jesus and appears to have been interchangeable with 'Christ', though it actually has the separate meaning of 'good'. Justin plays upon this (Apology 4). Suetonius or his source seems to have thought that Jesus was still alive.

Christ The anointed one (of God). The Greek title accorded to Jesus, corresponding with the Hebrew 'Messiah'.

Gnosticism The movement within early Christianity towards mystical, internal truths and explanations. The movement's name is derived from the Greek word for knowledge, and its followers sought to distinguish themselves from those who relied on faith and belief. The orthodox Christians' battle with the Gnostics is a central story of the first centuries of Christianity.

Heresy The followers of what was deemed – not necessarily at once – a heresy were those with an ultimately rejected point of view about an aspect or aspects of Christian belief. Christian heresy is virtually as old as Christianity. Gnosticism is the greatest of Christian heresies.

Jesus The Greek form of Joshua, meaning 'God delivers (or frees)'. The famous Old Testament Joshua, son of Nun, was not of his family. His family were proud of a descent from David of Bethlehem. But, curiously, Joshua was the minister and successor of Moses, brother of Aaron, from whom Elizabeth (Luke 1.5) – and therefore quite possibly Jesus' mother – could claim descent.

Messiah The anointed one, who would lead the Jews into a new era as their king (see the Mara bar Serapion text). Jesus seemed to take on this role – assisted in the minds of the people by a supposed descent from the old royal line. But his intentions were of a different order. After his departure from their lives the belief in the impending 'second coming' sustained Christians through a very dark period but probably turned into a deep source of disappointment for many – especially as events moved from bad to worse for the Jewish people.

Doubts seem to have developed about what form the second coming would take.

Nag Hammadi Library   A remarkable collection of some fifty Gnostic documents discovered in 1945. Much the most important is the Gospel of Thomas, of these the most nearly approaching mainstream Christianity as well as the authentic words of Jesus. The Dead Sea Scrolls, non-Christian documents also discovered in the twentieth-century, very shortly afterwards, must not be confused with these.

Son of Man   This mysterious title, not once queried by his listeners, is repeatedly used by Jesus for himself and never as a form of address to him. It is very probably an Aramaic* expression to be understood as a circumlocution for 'I' – much as we might jocularly say in English 'yours truly'. Some confusion may have developed with more esoteric meanings founded especially upon a prophetic dream in the Book of Daniel. (At 7.13 a 'son of man' is seen coming with the clouds of heaven into his imperishable kingdom.) It may also be considered whether this expression is a response to allegations of illegitimacy.

Synoptics   The three gospels of Matthew, Mark and Luke, of which Mark is very likely to be the first and Luke certainly the last. They 'readily admit of being brought under one combined view' – from a Greek word for 'seeing together'.

* That form of Semitic customarily spoken by Jesus and his followers.

NOTES

✞ The chi-rho symbol is a monogram of *chi* (X) and *rho* (P) as the first two letters of the Greek for Christ, *Kristos*.

INTRODUCTION (pp. 1–24)

p. 5   **1** Papias seems to have recognized this letter, along with Peter's first.

p. 5   **2** By Dionysius, Bishop of Alexandria.

p. 6   **3** Papias said, in his second book, that John was also killed by the Jews, according to the fifth-century Philip of Side.

p. 10   **4** Of three miracles recorded by Matthew but not Mark, Luke mentions one. Of twelve parables similarly, this fullest recorder of parables gives only two of Matthew's, while including three of Mark's four.

p. 12   **5** A third limitation is the desire to appeal to a gentile audience, even sometimes in the presentation of Jesus (as in Mark) as a scarcely Jewish figure.

p. 12   **6** It has been argued that John's gospel may have been assisted by 'John the Presbyter' – if he really existed. But it is easier to discount him altogether, despite real concerns over the single authorship of the Johannine documents. Papias would be a far more likely amanuensis, if Eusebius did not specifically record Papias' statement that he neither heard nor saw any of the apostles. Thus we may assume Papias came to Hierapolis after John's death, for Hierapolis and Ephesus were not far distant from each other. The argument against the second John, in brief, runs as follows: Papias as a young man went in search of the Christian truths as spoken by the leading Christians. He writes: 'But if at any time someone should come who had been in attendance on one of the elders I would carefully search out the elders' words – what Andrew or Peter had said or Philip, James, John, Matthew or any other of the Lord's disciples and what Aristion and the elder John, disciples of the lord, were [i.e. still] saying.' The elders are clearly the apostles, and in any case, if Papias was born *c.* 60 as we believe, why look for another John's words over the apostle John's who lived until *c.* 100?

p. 12 **7** But scholarly opinion is not inclined to see Peter's crucifixion as a prophecy, despite the likelihood of his coming to a violent end. It is also worth noting the failed prophecy that follows, i.e. Jesus' second coming would occur in John's lifetime.

p. 13 **8** The Chester Beatty manuscript, our earliest complete copy of the gospels, dates to *c.* AD 250.

p. 15 **9** R. Dunkerley, *Beyond the Gospels* (Penguin, 1957); from which a number of the following variants are taken.

p. 16   **10** There is a counter-argument that, for the reason given by Augustine, this passage was removed from many of our earliest gospel texts even though it is really by John. Another bone of contention is whether John's gospel, Papias, the Gospel of the Hebrews and the Armenian manuscript all actually refer to the same incident, one discrepancy being that adultery is not in all cases named as the woman's sin.

p. 17   **11** Ian Wilson, *Jesus: The Evidence* (HarperCollins, 1985), p. 60.

I: AN UNKNOWN GOSPEL (pp. 26–8)

p. 27   **1** The presence of these animals in this holy place is troublesome to scholars.

p. 27   **2** This expression 'prostitutes . . . and flute-girls' points to a link with the Gospel of the Nazareans, where the same expression is used in a version of the parable of the talents.

II: A SECOND UNKNOWN GOSPEL (pp. 30–33)

p. 31   **1** Various small losses in this and the following passages are supplied by scholarship, in part based upon the parallel texts within the canonical gospels.

III: THE GOSPEL OF THE EBIONITES (pp. 34–8)

p. 35   **1** Evidently, the second quartet of apostles has dropped out.

p. 36 **2** Though an account apparently derived from Hegesippus says that the Jerusalem Christians fled to Pella in AD 66, forewarned by an oracle.

IV: THE GOSPEL OF THE HEBREWS (pp. 40–44)

p. 42 **1** This act of healing was omitted by three of the four gospel-writers including apostles Matthew and John, though they all mention the wounding that preceded it.

p. 42 **2** Hegesippus distinguishes James the Just from the apostles; and during Jesus' ministry he seems to have been one of the doubting members of Jesus' family. Yet it is remarkable how James rose in the hierarchy after Jesus' death, if he were not an apostle. Clement of Alexandria claims that, with Peter and John, he was entrusted with the higher knowledge by Jesus, after the resurrection (Outlines, VI). But only Paul ever refers to James the Just as an apostle (Galatians 1.19) while nothing at all is known of James son of Alphaeus. Clement knew of 'the Just' and the son of Zebedee, and no other James.

p. 44 **3** Ignatius of Antioch. Letters 6 (to Smyrnaeans 3). This text is also referred to by Origen as from *The Preaching of Peter* (see 'Other Texts').

V: THE GOSPEL OF THE NAZAREANS (pp. 46–9)

p. 49 **1** This is another exaggeration.

VI: THE GOSPEL OF THE EGYPTIANS (pp. 50–52)

p. 50   **1** Their name derived from the Greek for self-restraint.

p. 51   **2** Compare Gospel of Thomas (22 and 37).

p. 52   **3** Confusingly, the author of the epistle is actually unknown, though this second-century homily is an important work, with a number of further quotations, of unidentifiable source. This author quotes a variant of the last saying introduced by the words 'Jesus . . . having been asked by someone when his kingdom would come . . .'

VII: THE GOSPEL OF THOMAS (pp. 54–72)

p55   **1** Didymos and Thomas mean the same (in Greek and Hebrew), i.e. twin. It is possible that Thomas was a twin, but, having the same first name as two others of Jesus' apostles, he was distinguished by this nickname.

p.56   **2** Eusebius and the sixth-century Decretum Gelasianum might also be mentioned if they are not referring to another Thomas gospel – there are several – but the important third-century Persian heretic Mani and/or his followers certainly knew the work, from which they quoted.

Saying 2   Versions in Pap. OX. 654 and in the Gospel of the Hebrews allow some such addition as: 'And when he has reigned, he will rest.'

Saying 4   The first portion of this is quoted in variant form by Hippolytus, who says the Naassene Gnostics cited it from the Gospel of Thomas.

Saying 5   Pap. OX. 654 adds, though the text is damaged: 'and nothing buried that will not be raised up'.

Saying 10   The Gnostic Pistis Sophia has a very similar saying.

Saying 11   'In the days . . .' Hippolytus has a similar saying cited from the Naassenes.

Saying 12   A witness to the importance of James the Just, future leader of the Jerusalem church. Epiphanius has Jesus entrusting his throne to James. This saying may come from the Gospel of the Hebrews.

Saying 17   This is cited by Paul (1 Corinthians 2.9), where it is not attributed to Jesus.

Saying 19   Irenaeus quotes the beginning in nearly the same words; likewise the Nag Hammadi Gospel of Philip. The five trees are frequently mentioned by the Gnostics.

Saying 22   'When you make the two into one . . .' See the Gospel of the Egyptians for another version of this.

Saying 27   Fasting from the world is referred to by Clement of Alexandria.

Saying 30   Pap. OX. 1 continues this saying with 'Raise up the stone and you will find me there. Split the piece of wood and I am there.'

Saying 37 See the Gospel of the Egyptians.

Saying 38 Irenaeus is one of many who offer a variant of this.

Saying 42 The famous variant on the mosque at Fathpur-Sikri in India is also found in the medieval author, Petrus Alphonsi. (See 'Miscellaneous Sayings of Jesus'.)

Saying 50 A strongly Gnostic text.

Saying 52 Augustine cites this from an heretical treatise but does not know its ultimate source (*Contra adv. legis et prophetarum* II.4).

Saying 61 This may be derived from the Gospel of the Egyptians.

Saying 74 Origen quotes a variant of this.

Saying 77 See note on Saying 30.

Saying 82 Origen quotes a close variant of this.

Saying 97 This parable is found only here.

Saying 98 Ditto as above.

Saying 101 Some such addition as 'gave me birth' or 'carried me in her womb' is probable.

Saying 105 Is this saying influenced by Jewish belief about Mary and Panthera?

Saying 111 'For Jesus says . . .' might be a later commentator's addition.

Saying 114 Hippolytus and Clement of Alexandria offer variants on this strange idea. It is possible that section 114 is an addition to the text, which may however simply reflect the idea in 106 (and 48) – the unification of the duality of gender explicit in the dialogue of Jesus and Salome (found in the Gospel of the Egyptians).

VIII: THE SECRET GOSPEL OF MARK (pp. 74–82)

p. 76   **1** A young man wearing only a linen cloth recurs at Mark 14.51–2.

p.78   **2** We are bound to wonder how this very private letter found its way into any collection of Clement's letters, if a collection is implied by the heading. And what happened to the rest?

p. 78   **3** Dr (afterwards Professor) Smith considered this second passage as perhaps a second-century addition. This seems implausible. It forms an odd antithesis to Luke 19.1–10, where Zacchaeus the rich tax collector, invited down by Jesus from his perch in a Jericho sycamore tree, 'received him joyfully'.

p. 78   **4** Where the absent text would fit after 'rest'.

p.78   **5** In fact, this argument could be improbably extended to propose that the abridged version was prepared at Alexandria after Mark's death. For the author is hardly likely to be responsible for awkward joins replacing missing texts. But how late could Mark's gospel be when clearly a source of Matthew and Luke's? Clement of

Rome, our earliest independent datable source, would seem to quote Mark once, in a variation of the parable of the sower.

p.79 **6** Perhaps Jesus was so angry with Salome for the folly of her recent request (Matt 20.20 ff) and the trouble it had caused among the other apostles (Matt 20.24) that he was not disposed to see her or those trying to mediate on her behalf.

IX: MISCELLANEOUS SAYINGS OF JESUS (pp. 84–7)

p. 85 **1** Note Clement's words in his letter on the Secret Gospel of Mark, that 'true matters blended together with fictions become false currency'.

p. 85 **2** R. Dunkerley, *Beyond the Gospels* (Penguin, 1957).

p. 86 **3** Dunkerley, op. cit.

p. 86 **4** Dunkerley, op. cit.

p. 87 **5** E. Hennecke, New Testament Apocrypha (SCM Press Ltd, 1973).

p. 87 **6** J. E. Hanauer, *Folk-Lore of the Holy Land*. (Duckworth 1907.

X: CLEMENT OF ROME'S SAYINGS OF JESUS (pp. 88–90)

p. 88 **1** Dio Cassius. Epit. 67.14.

p. 88 **2** Along with the 'Second Epistle of Clement' which however was written some half a century later and not by Clement. The following quotations from the Second Epistle should be noted:

> (1) And again he says, 'Woe to him who causes my name to be blasphemed'.

> (2) So then he says this, brother 'Guard the flesh to partake of the spirit.' Clement himself quotes especially from the Epistle to the Hebrews and I Corinthians, much less from the synoptics, once apparently from Acts (20.35), and never from John (who is first quoted from by Ignatius).

p. 89 **3** A strikingly similar passage is found in Polycarp's very early second-century Epistle to the Philippians, written shortly before Ignatius of Antioch's death – at least in its original form.

XI: QUADRATUS (pp. 92–3)

p. 92 **1** Quadratus' *Apology* has been thought possibly to survive nearly complete as *The Letter to Diognetus*, in which however, Eusebius' fragment is not included.

p. 93 **2** Philip of Side records Papias writing of people resurrected by Jesus living into the reign of Hadrian, emperor from 117. Presumably, one took the statement from the other: Quadratus and Papias wrote at nearly the same date.

XII: PAPIAS (pp. 94–6)

p. 94   **1** Since it is a source of confusion, *Papias never heard John directly*. Eusebius understood this from Papias' preface, despite the contrary evidence of Irenaeus (who should have known better) and other authorities.

p. 95   **2** An abbreviated version of this is given by Hippolytus.

XIII: HEGESIPPUS (pp. 98–103)

p. 98   **1** Probably the Gospel of the Nazareans.

p. 98   **2** Somewhat obscured in Luke's Acts.

p. 100   **3** In point of fact, the murder of Domitian in AD 96 – as a result of a plot involving his own wife – was the reason: he was replaced by the kindly Nerva who reversed his policy.

XIV: IRENAEUS (pp. 104–5)

p. 104   **1** In his *Letter to Florinus* Irenaeus records his memories of his elderly teacher. Polycarp wrote a surviving letter (to the Philippians) shortly before the death of Ignatius Bishop of Antioch who died *c.* 107. But there is a suspicion that this letter was later adapted. An eyewitness account of his martyrdom also survives.

p. 105   **2** An early Gnostic heretic whose ideas included the belief that Christ's coming kingdom would be on earth and offer an orgy of self-indulgence. The prologue to

John's Gospel has been said to take issue with his ideas. (See Caius in Eusebius C.H.III.28.)

XVI: JULIUS AFRICANUS (p. 112–14)

p. 113 **1** This has been identified with a village of virtually the same name, eight or ten miles north of Nazareth.

XVII: SAMUEL THE SMALL (p. 116–17)

p. 116 **1** Prayer of the heretics = Birkath haMinim.

p. 116 **2** Talmud, Gemara, Berakoth 28b–29a.

XVIII: BARCOCHBA (pp. 118–20)

p. 118 **1** Dio Cassius records over half a million Jewish dead, with fifty fortified towns and numerous villages razed to the ground.

p. 118 **2** Perhaps because he had his own Messianic tendencies. The alteration from Kosbah to Kochba (star) is interesting.

p. 119 **3** Other unpublished letters of Barcochba's have been mentioned recently as still extant. We must hope that their texts are made known.

XIX: TALMUD (pp. 122–6)

p. 123 **1** From the Tosefta, a supplement to the Talmud.

p. 124 **2** Perhaps the Gospel of Thomas 25 is closest of all, though only a variant of Zechariah 2.8

p. 124 **3** The first part is a variant of Micah 1.7.

p. 125 **4** See note 1.

XX: CELSUS (pp. 128–31)

p. 129 **1** Origen places a less detailed statement at this point, replaced here by a fuller version from later in the text. The early Christians attempted to present Panthera as an anagram of 'parthenos' (Greek for virgin).

p. 129 **2** The lost *Dialogue of Jason and Papiscus*, sometimes ascribed to Aristo of Pella, the main historian of Barcochba's rebellion, is an identifiable extra source for Celsus. (The fourth-century *Dialogue of Thomas and Aquila*, containing unusual early material, may be in part derived from this.)

p. 131 **3** Obviously Mary Magdalene.

XXI: JOSEPHUS (pp. 132–6)

p. 134 **1** That intelligent, decent, efficient procurator who presided at the Caesarea tribunal when Paul was brought before him (see Acts 25 and 26). His memorable words at 26.24 reveal the despair of an humane non-Christian.

p. 134 **2** This passage, known to both Origen and Eusebius but not in our surviving Josephus texts, is another indicator of the Josephus/Christianity problem.

p. 134   **3** Ian Wilson cites a text in the works of the tenth-century Arabic-Christian Agapius that might substantially represent the unadulterated version.

p. 135   **4** Josephus' other account indicates he intended to overpower the Roman garrison and set himself up as tyrant, under the protection of his followers.

p. 136   **5** In which he becomes conflated with Yeshu Ben Pantera despite their different names.

p. 136   **6** Celsus (Origen 1.68) names a long list of Egyptian magical practices conformable to the miracles ascribed to Jesus.

XXIII: TACITUS (pp. 140–41)

p. 140   **1** Nero may have had private reasons for his cruelty, for the Christians had infiltrated his own entourage. (See Paul's letter to the Philippians 4.22.) Another factor may have been Poppaea Sabina, his mistress from AD 58 and wife from AD 62. She was a great supporter of the Jews, and there is even a late story that Paul converted her. In the summer of AD 65, her husband gave her a savage kick while she was pregnant after she had complained about his late return from the games, and she died. A further factor might conceivably be Nero's secretary Epaphroditus if he could be identified with Paul's friend and helper sent by the Christians of Philippi in Macedonia, who is also mentioned in the above-named letter. R. Eisenman, who posits this identification, goes further in attempting to identify him with an important Jewish dedicatee of works of Josephus – also sharing the same name as the other two – of whom Josephus wrote, '[He] had a part in great events and many turns of fortune . . . showing . . . an immovable virtuous resolution in them all.' It remains a fascinating, tantalizing possibility. For this man (whose slave would be the Stoic Epictetus) would know intimately Paul, Nero, Josephus and Domitian, and perhaps Luke, Peter and Mark as well. See R. Eisenman, *James the Brother of Jesus* (Viking, 1997) the quotation is found at p. 639.

p. 140   **2** Suetonius refers to it as a 'new and mischievous superstition'.

p. 140   **3** Described as an alleged initiation ritual in horrid detail by the second-century Minucius Felix.

p. 140   **4** A misunderstanding or malign interpretation of the 'agape' or love-feast.

p. 140   **5** In Petronius' *Satyricon*, probably written shortly before AD 66, oblique allusion is perhaps made to this; for the millionaire Eumolpus will leave his wealth to his heirs only on the condition that they eat him.

XXIV: THE SLAVONIC VERSION OF JOSEPHUS (**pp. 142–5**)

p. 142   **1** This edition is referred to by Josephus in his preface.

p. 143   **2** A close correspondence here with an expression used in the *Antiquities* – see Josephus 2.

p. 144   **3** By G. A. Williamson, *Jospehus: The Jewish War*, trans., (Penguin, 1959).

p. 144   **4** A further text reveals efforts by successive 'excellent' procurators Cuspius Fadus and Tiberius Alexander, (who after Agrippa II's death governed from AD 44 to 48) to calm the situation by the killing of Christians. But Christian miracle-working deterred them, so that they left them alone until banishment and sending them abroad for trials were thought up as alternative solutions. The second procurator was an apostate Jew (see Acts 4.6), one of those who apparently tried to convince Vespasian that he was the one predicted to come from Judea to rule the world. Josephus and a famous rabbi also applied this important prophecy to Vespasian.

p. 145   **5** A variant text here says that Pilate had agreed to deliver Jesus to them.

p. 145   **6** See Matt 28.12–15 where the soldiers on guard took a bribe from the Jews to say that this had happened.

XXV: IMPERIAL POLICY (pp. 146–51)

p. 146   **1** This whole story might better suit Claudius (AD 41–54), whose first name was Tiberius.

p. 146   **2** Tiberius was dead before they could have met.

p. 146   **3** The name 'Christian' stemmed from Antioch, chief City of Syria.

p. 149   **4** A reference to the charge of cannibalism.

p. 149 **5** Under Roman law, the evidence of slaves was admissible only if they had been tortured.

p. 150 **6** Perhaps a response to Quadratus' or Aristides' *Apology*. This letter was written to the proconsul of Asia and preserved by Justin, who writes the introduction. It has been dated to *c.* 124.

XXVI: OTHER TEXTS (pp. 152–8)

p. 153 **1** Pseudo-ambrose.

p. 154 **2** J. W. Taylor's paraphrase in *The Coming of the Saints*. (Covenant, 1969).

p. 156 **3** The fourth-century philosopher Calcidius, in his commentary on Plato's Timaeus, mentions 'Wise men of the Chaldaeans' following a star that led them to a child-god recently born, to whom they offered worship. Celsus also refers to the coming of the Chaldaeans.

p. 156 **4** See Jeremiah, 41.7.

p. 156 **5** Which he said was where the followers of Tammuz (Adonis) mourned Tammuz's death. Tammuz was said to be buried on the heights above Bethlehem.

p. 157 **6** Later authorities, e.g. John Philoponus, deriving their knowledge from one or other of these, place it in the year an earthquake in Bithynia badly damaged Nicaea.

p. 158 **7** R. Dunkerley, *Beyond the Gospels*. (Penguin, 1957).

APPENDIX II: CHRISTIANITY AND THE FAMILY OF JESUS (pp. 165–8)

p. 165   **1** However an ingenious theory of Julius Africanus offers a way by which one or more of these might be uterine brother and sisters, with Cleophas as father. (See Luke 20.28.) This theory would presuppose Joseph's relatively early death, and Jesus not being considered as Joseph's son.

p. 165   **2** A short work on the apostles doubtfully ascribed to the third-century Hippolytus identifies James the Just with James the son of Alphaeus. It also lists Simon the son of Clopas and the second Bishop of Jerusalem as identical with Simon the Zealot. (But it may be unwise to place too much faith in this work as a reliable source.)

p. 165   **3** Compare Mark 15.40 and Matthew 27.56.

p. 165   **4** Matthew 20.20–28. Interestingly, the apocryphal Protevangelium names a Salome as present, just after Jesus' birth. Salome is also found with Mary Magdalene and Jesus' mother(?) in the Secret Gospel of Mark.

p. 166   **5** The Apostle Matthew is also referred to as son of Alphaeus.

p. 166   **6** Requested to look after Jesus' mother by Jesus – as 'the other' Mary and Cleophas were now old, and he was son of her sister? This request was made in front of Mary's sister (John.19.25–27).

p. 166   **7** It is not clear which was the more serious charge. Hegesippus also says that Symeon's accusers were arrested too – on the grounds of belonging to the same royal family.

p. 166   **8** I have elsewhere indicated the possibility that this was James – the more likely because of his greater (and perhaps controversial) significance, and Luke's failure in Acts to indicate his importance (see especially Acts 12.17 and 15.13 ff).

p. 166   **9** Herbert B. Workman, *Persecution in the Early Church*. (OUP, 1980).

APPENDIX III: DESCRIPTION OF JESUS (pp. 169–70)

p. 169   **1** 'Descendants' of this painting (destroyed by the Turks in 1453) are supposed to include *Our Lady of the Snows* in Santa Maria Maggiore at Rome, and *Our Lady of Czestochowa* in Poland.

p. 170   **2** Other writers also mention this statue, which John Malalas had discovered at the house of a converted Jew called Bassus. Macarius Magnes says the woman – Berenice or Veronica – came from Edessa (where also he seems to indicate the statue was). Sozomen tells how in the third century the great, humane anti-Christian emperor Julian commanded that it be taken down and replaced with a statue of himself. Christians recovered the remains after it had been desecrated by their opponents and placed it in a church where it was still preserved.

APPENDIX IV: CHRONOLOGY (pp.171–4)

p. 171   **1** These dates, hinging on events recorded only in Matthew, are hugely doubtful. The Massacre of the Innocents may not have occurred in fact or even been rumoured *at that time*, though some babies' skeletons have been found at Jerusalem in modern times, supposedly dating from the same period. Luke rejected Matthew's story, but his own story of the nativity seems too late, if we accept that he was referring to Quirinius' census (AD 6) as the reason for Jesus' birth in Bethlehem, though Justin (Apology 34) insists that Quirinius' census confirms the birth. Perhaps it did – *but not for that date*. It is anyway unlikely the census would have required the family to go to Bethlehem, rather than Sepphoris. Jesus' birth may have been shortly before or after Herod's death but, on balance of probabilities, it was before. Herod the Great, a powerful character and able king, was too despotic to win popularity despite huge largesse (including the Temple at Jerusalem). In his last years he declined partly (one suspects) because of failing health. He may have developed cancer of the bowels. But he was surrounded by intriguers within his own family, among whom his sister Salome was responsible for the execution of his favourite wife, Mariamne; and Mariamne's two sons, embittered against him, were also executed in 7 BC. Another intriguer, his eldest son Antipater, of whom he was very fond, was also executed in the last days of Herod's life.

The Roman Governor of Syria, Saturninus (9–6 BC) – Tertullian believed he conducted a census and G. A. Williamson refers to an inscription dated to 8 BC, naming an earlier registration, though client-states were not liable to census – had urged mercy for Mariamnes' sons. And the emperor Augustus, once on friendliest terms, is supposed to have said, 'Better to be Herod's pig than his son.'

This weary, sick and disappointed old man might have felt threatened by the old rival dynasty of David or responded to ostensible prophecy. We simply do not know. But unquestionably he passed into legend, and many stories were told about him.

p. 172 **2** Described by Jesus as 'that fox' (Luke 13.32) after the Pharisees reported that Antipas would kill him. Antipas is always referred to as Herod in the New Testament.

SOURCES OF MAIN TEXTS

UNKNOWN Pap. Oxyrhynchus 840

UNKNOWN 2 Pap. Egerton 2

EBIONITES Epiphanius Adv. Haereses 30

HEBREWS 1) Cyril of Jerusalem
2) Jerome. Commentary on Isaiah 4
3) Origen on John 2.12.87
4) Jerome. Commentary on Eph 5.4
5) Jerome. Commentary on Ezek 18.7
6) Jerome. De Vir. Inl 2

NAZAREANS 1) Sedulius Scotus. Commentary on Matthew
2–3) Jerome. Dial.adv. Pel III.2
4) Origen. Comm on Matt XV
5) Jerome. Ep CXX

EGYPTIANS Clement of Alexandria. Strom. III

THOMAS   Nag Hammadi Library Cod II.2

SECRET GOSPEL OF MARK
              ?Letter of Clement of Alexandria to Theodorus

SAYINGS
              1) Epiph. Adv. Haer. 44.2
              2) Justin Dial. 35.3
              3) Clem Alex. Strom. 1.24.158
              4) Apostolic Gospel 26
              5) Tertullian on Baptism 20
              6) Ephraem Syrus Comm. on Gospels
              7) Clem. Hom. X1X.20.2
              8) Clem. Alex. Exc. E Theodoto 1.2.2
              9) Second Epistle of Clement 4

CLEMENT OF ROME
              First Epistle

QUADRATUS Eusebius, Church History, IV.3

PAPIAS   Irenaeus. Adv. Haereses 5.33–4

HEGESIPPUS Eusebius. Church History,
              1) II.23
              2) III.12
              3) III.20

CLEMENT OF ALEXANDRIA
              Eusebius C.H. III.23

IRENAEUS   Eusebius C.H. IV.14

JULIUS AFRICANUS
          Eusebius C.H. I.7

SAMUEL THE SMALL
          Twelfth of the eighteen Benedictions (version in
          the Cairo Genizah)

BARCOCHBA Letter to Yeshua ben Galgolah

TALMUD AND TOSEFTA
          Mishnah Yebamoth 49a
          Talmud (Gemara) Sanhedrin 43a
          Talmud (Gemara) Sanhedrin 43a
          Talmud (Gemara) Gittin 57a
          Tosefta Yebamoth 3–4
          Talmud (Gemara) 'Abodah Zarah 16b
          Tosefta Chulin 2.22

CELSUS   Origen contra Celsum I and II (Description of Jesus
          is found at VI.75)

JOSEPHUS
          1) Eusebius C.H. II.23 (from Antiquities xx)
          2) Eusebius C.H. II.11 (from Antiquities xviii)
          3) Antiquities XX.169–72

SUETONIUS   Life of Claudius XXV.4

TACITUS   Annals XV.44

JOSEPHUS: SLAVONIC TEXT
        See, for example, Josephus' Jewish War and its
        Slavonic Version (Brill, 2003), by Leeming,
        Leeming and Osinkina

PLINY/TRAJAN
        Letters of Pliny the Younger X, 96 and 97

HADRIAN   Eusebius C.H. IV.9 (from Justin. Apology)

FURTHER READING

Early Christian Writings (Translated M. Staniforth), Penguin Books, 1968

Eusebius, *The History of the Church* (Translated G. A. Williamson), Penguin Books, 1961

Hennecke, E., *New Testament Apocrypha* (Translated 1963), SCM Press Ltd, 1973

James, M. R., *The Apocryphal New Testament*, OUP, 1926

Stevenson, J., *A New Eusebius*, S.P.C.K., 1957

Vermes, G., *The Authentic Gospel of Jesus*, Penguin Books, 2004 (and all other Christian writings of this great scholar)

Wilson, A. N., *Jesus*, Sinclair-Stevenson Ltd, 1992

Wilson, Ian, *Jesus, the Evidence*, Weidenfeld & Nicolson, 1984

INDEX

Note: Significant treatment of a subject is indicated by page numbers in bold.

209